They Still Serve

The Complete Guide to the Military Ghosts of Britain

They Still Serve

The Complete Guide to the Military Ghosts of Britain

By

Richard McKenzie

Lulu.com

2008

First Published in 2008
By lulu.com
Copyright ©Richard McKenzie 2008
ISBN: 978-1-4092-0137-3

CONTENTS

Introduction	9
Prehistoric	12
Romans	14
Saxons	26
Vikings	29
Medieval	33
17th Century	53
18th & 19th Century	83
First World War	95
Between the Wars	101
Second World War	102
Unknown Ghosts	128
Bibliography	132
Index	136

Introduction

This guide is the by-product of more than 20 years of interest in the subject of ghosts and hauntings. As a child I was fascinated by the terror that such tales would bring and many were the nights that I lay awake underneath my duvet convinced that some unknown horror was in my room waiting to get me if I left the protection of my covers. Later as my interest in history grew I started to look at the stories from a more critical angle and quickly came to realise that there were simply too many sightings for the whole idea of ghosts to be dismissed as superstition. Now after researching this book I have come to the conclusion that there do seem to be areas in Britain where incidents from the past were recorded into the atmosphere and these can be re-played in the right circumstances, the so called 'stone tape theory.'

In writing this guide I am not attempting to understand the phenomenon that is the paranormal, nor am I attempting to answer any questions as to the nature of ghosts or the viability of their sightings. Instead I am simply cataloguing those areas of Britain where so far inexplicable events have occurred. What they are and how they have come about I will leave to others more qualified than I to discuss.

I have broken this guide into chapters dealing with periods of history and the sightings that have been recorded, rather than geographical locations, as I feel this is the easiest way to deal with the large numbers of haunting I will be discussing.

I wish to thank Mr Peter Underwood for getting me interested in the subject via his many books on ghosts, my teachers at Pocklington school, in particular Mr Solomon, whose passion for history rubbed off on me, and my father for paving the way in my family by his writing and for encouraging me to write myself. This book is the creation of all their combined efforts, though it goes without saying that any mistakes in the work are mine and not theirs.

TO MY FAMILY

FOR ENCOURAGING ME

EVEN WHEN I DIDN'T KNOW WHERE I WAS GOING

Prehistoric

This period covers a vast time frame from the Palaeolithic, the Old Stone Age, through to the coming of the Romans in 43 AD when Britain reached the Historic Period. Given the timescale involved it is interesting that I have only managed to unearth four examples of warrior ghosts from this period.

Badbury Rings, Dorset

Here there are the remains of a well preserved Iron Age hillfort. On certain nights the ghost of a warrior on horseback is said to be seen. Some have claimed that this is the spirit of King Arthur, but it is more likely that it is the ghost of an unknown soldier still guarding the fort as he must have done over two thousand years ago.

Bottlebrush Down, Dorset

In 1924 Mr Clay, an archaeologist who was involved in a Bronze Age excavation at Christchurch, was driving home. Just as he came to an area where the old Roman road crossed the A3081 he became aware of a horseman galloping towards him. The figure stayed parallel with the car for some time and so Mr Clay was able to observe it for a considerable period, something most ghost hunters do not get the chance to do. He described the figure as having bare legs, a long flowing cloak, and a weapon which he brandished over his head. The horse was smallish and was being ridden bareback without bridle or stirrups. After staying with the startled archaeologist for some 100 yards or so the rider and horse suddenly disappeared. The next day Mr Clay returned to the area where the figure had disappeared and found the remains of a barrow, or Bronze Age burial mound, which had been destroyed by ploughing. Given his knowledge of the period Mr Clay dated the ghost to the late Bronze Age, sometime around 700 BC.

Chysauster, Cornwall

This is the remains of one of the best preserved Iron Age villages in Britain and it is thought to have been occupied from 100 BC to 300 AD. The site is a lonely one, though there is no need to feel lonely when you are there for, if rumour is correct, you will share your visit with the ghosts of several smallish men who have been seen from time to time in the village and are thought to be the spirits of the original settlers.

West Tump Barrow, Gloucestershire

A female witness claimed to have seen four men dressed in ancient clothing wielding Stone Age weapons standing on the hill. So far this remarkable sighting has been seen only once and as such it is impossible to date the ghosts accurately. The suggestion that the warriors had Stone Age weapons does not help much for these would have been as common in the Early Bronze Age as they were in the Stone Age.

The Roman Period

The Romans first appeared on our shores, in a military capacity, in 55 and 54 BC when Julius Caesar launched two expeditions, supposedly to punish the Britons for helping their fellow Celts resist the Roman expansion in Gaul. After these incursions our shores were left unmolested for nearly a century, until 43 AD when the Roman emperor Claudius, desperate for a military victory to shore up his claim to the Imperial throne, launched his successful invasion of Britain. For the next three hundred and sixty or so years the Romans occupied England and Wales, periodically pacified and attempted to occupy Scotland at various times. The Romans influenced more than just our architecture, laws and customs, they also appear to have influenced our supernatural heritage for there have been literally dozens of reported sightings of ghostly Roman armies and individual soldiers throughout the length and breadth of Great Britain.

Ardoch, Perthshire, Scotland

This is one of the largest and best preserved timber forts in Britain and is famous for its earthwork defences. Here, where tradition states the Romans buried a great treasure as they prepared to leave Scotland, a phantom Roman army has been seen in the location marching away on an unknown mission.

Bindon Hill, Dorset

Here, an army which marches over the hill from Flowers Barrow has been seen.

Bonchester Bridge, Peeblesshire, Scotland

Soldiers have been seen marching down the A6088 towards the remains of the Roman fort of Chesters.

Bowerchalke, Wiltshire

The sounds of fierce fighting and the ghosts of headless horses are said by tradition to mark the site of a battle between Romans and Britons.

Burton Constable Hall, Hull

Phantom Roman soldiers are said to march across the parkland along a lost Roman road.

Chanctonbury Ring, Washington, Sussex

Along with other ghosts, including an old man with a long flowing white beard and the sound of pounding hooves, said to date from Caesar's assault on the hillfort, the ghosts of druids can be summoned if you run around the fort seven times at midnight.

Chester Green, Derby

The area is said to be haunted by the ghosts of a Roman army but so far witnesses only recount sighting a single soldier.

Corbridge, Northumberland

This site was known as Corstopitum in Roman times, and Roman soldiers have occasionally been seen. In 1777 Frances Murray from Leith was visiting friends in the area when he saw a Roman army march across the nearby hillside and disappear in a copse of trees. Much more recently a witness from Newcastle, also visiting friends saw the ghost of a Roman Legionary standing on guard.

Glossop, Derbyshire

Here an army which appears to be setting off from the Roman fort at nearby Melandra Castle has been seen; some traditions have it that this legion is carrying burning torches. Nearby in a bend in the road which connects Glossop to Woodhead the ghost of a single Roman soldier has been seen along with other spirits.

Honeypot Lane, Stanmore, London

The ghostly noise of a great rushing sound and the awful feeling that something terrible is creeping up behind you is said to be a psychic echo of a great battle fought here between Caesar's army and the defending Britons.

Kilmington, East Devon

There have been repeated sightings of Roman soldiers marching away from the main road towards a disused trackway which was part of the Roman road from Dorchester to Exeter. This sighting is traditionally seen on the eve of midsummer.

Packman Lane, Kiveton Park, Rotherham

Roman soldiers are said to march along on their knees, due to the road surface being lower in their day, but they only appear on nights of strong moonlight.

RAF Valley, Anglesey

The ghosts of Roman soldiers have been seen marching around the perimeter of this RAF base, but so far no archaeological reason has been put forward as to why they are there.

Roman Steps, Llyn Cwm Bychan, Gwynedd, Wales

The ghosts of Roman miners and soldiers have been seen ascending and descending.

The Ridgeway

Above Weymouth, Roman soldiers have been seen marching, but only at times of national emergency.

Similar sightings of Roman soldiers have been recorded at **Danbury, Essex**; **Bitterne Manor, Southampton**, where Roman soldiers are said to patrol this part of the city; **Wecock Farm, Hampshire**; **Malvern Hills, Hereford and Worcester**; **Penwortham Hill, Lancashire**; **Littlecote Park, Wiltshire**; **Oldbury Camp, Wiltshire** and finally **Gop Carn, Trelawnyd**.

Abbey Church, Bath

Tradition states that the naked ghost of a Roman soldier has been seen running around the centre of the town. It is said that a police officer once gave chase to the phantom streaker only to watch it fade into nothing. The point has to be made though as to how the witnesses know the nationality of this phantom without it having any clothes to provide clues.

Ambresbury Hillfort, Essex

Here, some claim, Boudicca was buried. She led the Britons resistance to Roman occupation in 60/61 AD and so nearly kicked them out of their newly conquered province. Her ghost has been seen at this spot from time to time.

Bowes, Barnard Castle

Tradition tells us that there was a Roman fort here and that when the legions left Britain, at the beginning of the fifth century AD, the Roman garrison looted the houses of the citizens living nearby and then buried their stolen treasure. Angered by this act the natives massacred the Romans before they could leave. The ghosts of the slaughtered garrison are said to be periodically seen in the act of burying their treasure.

Bradwell on Sea, Essex

One of the earliest churches founded in England still stands in the ruins of a Roman fort. The ghost of a soldier has been seen marching from Weymarks Farm to the 7th century church of St Peters. This may be the same ghost who is heard galloping through locked gates from the nearby village to the church.

Burgh Castle, Norfolk

This is one of the Saxon Shore Forts, it also has a psychic echo from this period. Once a year the sounds of battle are heard echoing through the ruin which is said to be a re-enactment of a fight between Roman soldiers and Saxon raiders.

Caerleon Campus, Newport, Gwent, Wales

This Campus is haunted by a Roman soldier probably because the building was built on the site of a Roman cemetery.

Cammeringham, Lincolnshire

Local tradition has it that Boudicca's last battle was fought here and her spirit, in a ghostly chariot, has been seen.

Chester, Cheshire

A soldier has been sighted and heard frequently over the last 100 years marching along the well preserved walls that once protected him and his garrison.

Chingle Hall, Longridge

This fine building is claimed to be one of the most haunted sites in Britain. Twenty spectres are supposed to reside within its walls including the ghost of a Roman centurion, though why he should haunt this particular building is not clear.

Coombe Dingle Bridge, Somerset

Here one lady claimed to have seen a Roman soldier on several occasions.

Denbigh Moors, Denbigh & Stone Bridge, Plas Pren, Wales

Both of these places are home to ill-omened Roman soldiers which, if sighted, will lead to the witnesses death soon after.

Dover Castle, Kent

The Roman Pharos, or lighthouse, has the ghost of a Roman soldier who appears to eternally keep watch.

George and Dragon Inn, Chester

This pub was built over three hundred years ago on the site of a Roman burial ground 500 yards from the city walls. The ghost of a Roman sentry is said to walk the upper floors. A steady tread of footsteps can be heard pacing to one end and returning twenty minutes later, always in the small hours of the morning.

Girton College, Cambridge

A Roman centurion was seen briefly when the college was first built, though he has been quiet of late.

Gisleham, Suffolk

Here the noise of a skirmish is heard, said to date from the early fifth century when the legions were leaving Britain's shores.

Lympne Castle, Kent

Still on patrol is the Roman soldier who fell to his death from one of the towers of this castle which was formerly a Roman fortress. His ghostly wanderings are shared by the spirits of six Saxon soldiers who were killed here by invading Normans after the battle of Hastings in 1066.

M6 Toll Road, Lichfield, Staffordshire

Here in December 2005 a family driving home saw what they first interpreted as animals crossing the road. As they drew nearer they soon realised that what they were seeing were not animals, but Roman soldiers marching waist deep through the tarmac. Lichfield did have a strong Roman presence historically and it is highly likely that Roman soldiers would have marched frequently in the area where this fascinating account comes from.

Milecastle 42, Hadrian's Wall, Northumbria

Here tradition relates that the spirit of a Roman auxiliary soldier who having fallen in love with a young native girl, was betrayed by her and committed suicide after finding out. He has been seen and heard on his lonely patrol, still guarding the wall he swore to protect all those years ago.

Monks Park area, Corsham

A private residence in this area is supposed to be haunted by a Roman soldier, though this shade has not been seen for some time.

Moresby Hall, Whitehaven, Cumbria

Three Roman soldiers have been sighted here over the last century though again their reason for residing in the hall is unknown.

North Tidworth, Wiltshire

Whether there is the ghost of Roman soldier here is not clear for some witnesses have described him as looking more like a highlander in a kilt.

Richborough Castle, Kent

The ghosts of several Roman soldiers have been seen.

Slaybrook Corner, Saltwood, Kent

An appropriately named site where reputedly an ancient battle took place and where the ghost of a Roman soldier has been seen. However, this interpretation is open to dispute for some claim the ghost that haunts this area is in fact William Tournay, an eccentric local landowner, whose body is buried in an island on the nearby lake.

The Castle Public House, Chichester

Another town with strong Roman connections. Here a Roman soldier is reported to enter the pub after first walking the boundary of the old city wall. It is not known, however, if this is the same entity as the one blamed for the disruption in the pub's loft which is reported from time to time.

The Dales, Ipswich

The Dales saw in the 1980's, a spate of reports of a Roman soldier being seen by some nearby trees.

The Strood, Mersea Island, Essex

Tradition has it that you can hear not only the sounds of this Roman soldier's hobnailed boots but also the noises of screams and clashing swords, the psychic echo of a forgotten battle fought long ago. One witness recounted how the soldier had followed her from Mersea Barrow to the Causeway and that when her friend joined her she too could hear the sound of his footsteps. In February 1970 two men driving in the area reported sighting a man surrounded by a white mist, possibly the soldier but equally likely another unknown spirit.

Theydon Bois Hillfort, Epping Forest

Boudicca's spirit is said to appear here as well, along with her daughters.

Thor's Cave, Derbyshire

A centurion is said to guard the mouth of the cave.

Treasurer's House, York

In 1953 a young plumber's apprentice, Harry Martindale, was working in the cellars when he heard a blast from a trumpet. As the noise got nearer he saw, as he fell from his ladder in surprise, a Roman officer on horseback emerging from the wall, followed by a line of soldiers, all wearing green tunics, stumbling wearily along behind their leader. This proved too much for the poor man who fled from the cellar in terror. It emerged later that the Treasurer's House does indeed lie on a Roman road and that what Harry saw that day were most likely Roman auxiliaries coming home after a long march. This is not the only time that the Roman soldiers have been seen on this site. Earlier in the century the house belonged to Mr Frank Green who one day held a fancy dress ball. One of his guests later complained to him about another of the guests, dressed as a Roman soldier, who had rudely barred her from entering one of the cellars by blocking her way with his spear or pilum. Needless to say when Mr Green later checked it was found that no guest had come as a Roman soldier that night.

Wath Wood Hospital, Wath upon Dearne, Yorkshire

Home to a Roman soldier who would check on all new admissions as they slept.

Woodchester Mansion, Stroud

The parkland is said to be home to a Roman soldier.

Wroxham, Norfolk

Here on 13th and 16th April, the 2nd and 21st May, the 1st, 4th and 11th June, the 5th 13th and 19th August, the 13th, 15th and 22nd September and finally the 7th and 9th October, you might be lucky to see the ghost of a Roman soldier who will brusquely order you out of the way. The reason for his rudeness soon becomes clear for he is clearing the way for a ghostly procession of horses, lions, chariots, soldiers, prisoners and gladiators who are all making their way from the Roman fort at Brancaster to the nearby amphitheatre. This is truly a unique, and one would have thought unforgettable, experience for any who witness it.

York between Church Street and Davygate

In 1958 two women briefly saw a battle between Roman troops and barbarians before a van drove by, obscuring their view, and the whole scene vanished.

The Saxons

With the evacuation of the Roman army, and the ordering by the Emperor Honorius that Britain must now look to her own defence rather rely on the embattled Romans desperately fighting to maintain the western Empire, we enter the age of the Anglo – Saxons. From c.410 – 1066 England was occupied by invading waves of Angles, Saxons and Jutes who collectively became Anglo – Saxon, and gave England her name. Despite their longer occupation of these lands than the Romans they have left far fewer traces of themselves on our spectral heritage, though there are some sites which can claim a Saxon ghost or two.

Bloodmoor Hill, Suffolk

The site of a skirmish, probably in the middle of the fifth century AD between the invading Angles and the defending Romano – British, the British were routed and slaughtered and the sounds of their screams, as well as the general din of battle, are said to resound in the area of the conflict.

Burnham Green, Hertfordshire

The ghosts of several galloping horses are said to be spirits of the slain, killed in an unknown battle over a thousand years ago.

Dacre Castle, Cumbria

This site has the ghosts of three Saxon thanes, who, tradition tells us, are meeting to discuss the Viking threat in the ninth century which came so close to overwhelming Anglo Saxon England.

Dunnichen, Angus, Scotland

In January 1950 a woman walking home late witnessed the aftermath of a battle fought over 1300 years earlier. She saw men dressed in ancient clothing searching through corpses which littered the area as far as she could see. The area, known to the English as Nechtansmere, was the site of a battle fought between the Picts and the Northumbrian Saxons who had occupied lowland Scotland. The Picts won the battle, the first the Scottish people would fight in a long war for their independence from England.

Heydon Ditch, Cambridgeshire

This is an earthwork which stretches for three miles from Heydon to Fowlmere. The site is said to be haunted by the ghosts of giant Saxon warriors. This idea was given credence in the 1950's when an archaeological excavation revealed the graves of several Saxon warriors in the vicinity where the ghosts were reported.

Hope Valley, Derbyshire

The site of another Saxon battle, this time fought between the kingdoms of Wessex and Northumbria and the sounds of that battle can still be heard to this day.

Horning, Norfolk

At this site it is said that every five years on 21st July you can witness the ghostly re-enactment of the crowning of Ella, an early king of the Angles, by the Abbot of St Bennets. Traditionally the best site from which to witness this magical display is about 100 yards downstream from the Swan Inn, on the opposite side of the river.

St Andrew's Church, Ashingdon, Essex

The hill on which the church was built is said to have been a battlesite where the blood ran so thick grass could not grow, though the hill is grassy nowadays. The ghostly moans heard on the hill and in the church are said to be from the wounded and dying on that bloody day

The Vikings

From their first raid on British soil, at Lindisfarne in 793, to their final battle, and defeat, at Largs in 1263, the Vikings terrorised Britain. First coming as hit and run raiders their tactics had changed by the ninth century and a large invasion force quickly conquered the Kingdoms of Northumbria, Mercia and East Anglia. At the same time the Vikings were carving territories out for themselves in the north and west of Scotland and northern and central Ireland. In England only Wessex with its young King Alfred was left of the Saxon kingdoms. Alfred managed to defeat the Viking army under its commander Guthrum at the battle of Eddington in 878 and so ensured Saxon survival. So powerful though were the northmen that Alfred was forced to partition the country into the lands occupied by the Vikings, called The Danelaw and the Saxon lands. Gradually Alfred's successors, Edward the Elder and Athelstan reconquered much of the Danelaw only to have Ethelred the Unready lose it all again to a further wave of Viking attacks. This paved the way for the crowning of the Viking King Canute, who died in 1034 and was to prove the highpoint for the Viking Age. After the swift removal and death of Canute's successors they were never again to sit on a British throne though they were still threatening to do so when William the Conqueror took the throne in 1066. This legacy of raiding and battle still survives in the ghostly annals of Britain and in fact there are more sites associated with Viking ghosts than there are Saxon ones. Perhaps telling us something of the terror they inspired in the native inhabitants of this land.

Canvey Island, Essex

The ghost of a Viking warrior has been seen and is said to be the spirit of a man killed in 894 AD when Edward the Elder routed a pillaging Viking warband.

Dent, Cumbria

Here the ghosts of dozens of Vikings on horseback have been witnessed.

Dowsborough, Somerset

Tradition says that there was a Danish camp that was attacked successfully by a Saxon army. The sounds of carousing and fighting have been heard in the vicinity as well as the voice of a singing child, said to be a Danish child spared by the Anglo-Saxons when they attacked the camp.

Gainsborough Old Hall, Lincolnshire

This hall is said to be built on an old Saxon fort which was attacked by a Viking force from Denmark. The Danes were beaten off and their leader was killed. The groaning sounds heard infrequently here are said to be the noises of the dying Viking leader.

Iona

Regarded as the heart of Scottish Christianity this monastery was raided several times in the eighth and ninth centuries and many monks were killed. It is said that from time to time you can see these raids re-enacted as ghostly Viking vessels sail silently onto the shore and Viking warriors scramble out.

Kingley Vale, Sussex

This is traditionally the site of a battle fought sometime in the ninth or tenth centuries, the tradition is not too clear on this point. What it is clear about though is the fact that the site is haunted by the ghosts of the slain, both Saxon and Vikings.

Ludham Bridge, Norfolk

On 2nd April every year a small group of Vikings are said to appear heading towards the bridge, some of them blowing horns.

South Walsham in Norfolk

Here every year there is said to be a re-enactment of a pagan Viking funeral. Witnesses report sighting a longship carrying the body of a Viking warlord being set alight around a crowd of Viking warriors.

Spanish Head, the Isle of Man

During the reign of the Viking King of Man Olaf I twenty four men were sent by Olaf's nephew to kill him but they failed and were beheaded for their crimes. The ghosts of these men are seen occasionally looking for their heads in this area.

St Savour's Church, York

The spirit of an executed Viking warrior is supposed to haunt this church. He must be a truly terrifying site for local rumour has it that a ghost hunter once spent the night here hoping to witness the ghost. The vicar calling on the man the next morning found him high up on a beam dead from fright.

Tutt Hill, Suffolk

The noises of fighting and a man screaming have been heard over the years. The fighting is said to date from the Viking attack on the town of Thetford which was successfully taken by them. As for the screaming man, tradition tells us that he was a Saxon traitor who betrayed Thetford to the Vikings and was rewarded for his efforts by being executed by his victorious 'allies.'

The Medieval Period

With the coming of the Normans in 1066 Britain enters the High Middle Ages. From now on the ghosts we encounter can be found in the castles, fortified manor houses and grand churches which so adorn our countryside, as well, of course as the usual battlefields, lonely moors and even the odd hotel. From 1066 to the coming of the Tudors in 1485 the Kingdoms of England and Scotland, though so often at war with each other, grew rich on trade and spent that money constructing fortified symbols of power to show of their influence. It is no wonder that in some cases the ghostly architects of these buildings have been so very reluctant to leave their former homes.

Ardrossan Castle, Ayrshire, Scotland

During the Scottish Wars of Independence William Wallace slaughtered the English garrison of the castle and piled their bodies in the cellar, morbidly known as Wallace's larder. Perhaps he later came to repent of this bloody deed for the ghost of this famous freedom fighter has been seen on occasions in the castle.

Baconsthorpe Castle, Norfolk

The ghost seen here is said to be a medieval soldier still on patrol. He is usually seen on the battlements and has been blamed for the occasional stone cast into the moat when visitors are near.

Bamburgh Castle, Northumbria

Said to be haunted by the ghost of a medieval knight who appears to favour the 12th century keep for his wanderings. One night a young lady, asleep in this part of the castle, saw the spirit appear in her room, cross it, and exit out of her door into the corridor. Another spirit seen in the castle is that of an Elizabethan naval gunner who, it is claimed, has a particularly cheeky grin.

Battle Abbey, Sussex

The ghost of King Harold Godwinson, who was killed at the Battle of Hastings, 1066, is said to appear in the ruins of this site. The altar of the abbey was built on the spot where he died. His ghost is of course seen with the obligatory arrow in the eye.

Berkley Castle, Gloucestershire

This castle is haunted by ghostly noises though this time it is known who is responsible. For it was here on 21st September 1327 that Edward II suffered the agonising death of *cum vero ignite inter celanda confossus* or a red hot poker inserted into his rectum. His screams are said to resound throughout the castle on the anniversary of his murder.

Berry Pomeroy Castle, Devon

The ruins of this castle are haunted by several spectres; the earliest and most famous is that of Sir Henry de Pomeroy. He supported Prince John in his attempt to wrest the throne of England from Richard the Lionheart, while the latter was imprisoned during his return from the Third Crusade. When he heard that Richard had been freed and was coming home Henry ordered his horse to be made ready, blindfolded it, and then rode it over the northern wall of the castle. It is said that on certain nights of the year you can hear the noise of Henry urging his horse on, and the sound of them both falling to their deaths.

Berwick on Tweed

At the beginning of the Scottish Wars of Independence King Edward I of England laid siege to this port town. At this time Berwick belonged to the Scottish throne and was her most prosperous port. Edward's declaration that the town could surrender without fear of sack was greeted with insolence by the town's defenders, some of whom bared their breeches at him. As it turned out the defenders should not have been so confident, for their town's defences were sorely in need of repair. Angered by the townsfolk Edward ordered an immediate assault and within one hour the town, though not the castle, was in his hands. The King then commanded that the women and children be allowed to leave and then allowed his men to sack the town and massacre all the men folk. Such were the rules of war in the medieval period. This brutal sacking has left spirits behind in the town. In August 1981 a woman on holiday in the area saw a small group of around 20 men fighting with sword and claymore close to the river. On going to the Tourist Information Office to enquire about any re-enactment groups in the area she was of course told that there were none. In 1958 an American tourist visiting the castle was horrified to find herself in the middle of a battle. All around her were the sounds of swords clashing on armour, at one point she even felt that she had been splashed with blood. Unsurprisingly she quickly left the scene.

Blackness Castle, West Lothian, Scotland

Here a ghostly knight on horseback rushed at a tourist forcing the terrified young man to flee.

Bolton Priory, Wharfedale, Yorkshire

In the spring of 1973, several amateur archaeologists called off their search for the grave of Sir John de Clifford, who was killed during the Wars of the Roses, after frightening events occurred. On one occasion a female member of the archaeological team was confronted by the ghost of a man in a medieval costume, whilst on another occasion another member was terrified by the vision of something dark and evil emanating from a tomb they were excavating.

Bracebridge Hall and Church, Lincolnshire

These connected sites are haunted by the ghost of a local knight who was buried in the nearby churchyard. His spirit is said to materialise in the hall, and then ride on horseback to the graveyard in order to ensure that his body has not been disturbed. His ghost has also been seen from time to time in the church itself.

Bramham Moor, York

A battle was fought here on 19th February 1408 between the rebel army of Lord Percy and the royalist army commanded by Sir Thomas Rokeby. Percy was defeated, captured and executed. The phantom sounds of the battle have been heard in the area from time to time.

Burwell Castle, Cambridgeshire

Here the ghost of a De Mandeville has been seen. He was killed whilst trying to storm the castle at the head of a levied army of thieves and robbers.

Byward Tower, Tower of London

In the 1980's a yeoman warder doing his rounds entered one of the rooms and was startled to see two beefeaters dressed in an earlier style of clothing, smoking and conversing on either side of the fireplace. As the warder stared at them one of the beefeaters turned, stared back at him and then the scene vanished

Castlemilk, Glasgow, Scotland

This site has been mostly demolished but in one of the few rooms left, the ghost of a medieval soldier has been seen wandering. This is a ghost to be wary, of for tradition says that this spirit once shot an arrow into the back of the head of a local man who needed several stitches to close his wound.

Chillingham Castle, Northumbria

Another Northumbrian Castle with a ghost. This time it is the spirit of a medieval warrior who staggers up to the main entrance carrying a full quiver of arrows on his back before vanishing. According to tradition he is eternally bringing a warning, to the lord of the castle, of an impending Scottish attack.

Chingle Hall, Longridge

This site we encountered earlier when we spoke about Roman soldiers, but here also the spirit of a knight in armour has been seen. This mysterious place keeps it secrets well, for of the many ghosts known to haunt it few of them can be traced to a definite event or have a reason to do so.

Croft Castle, Hereford and Worcester

This ghost, claimed to be the Welsh resistance fighter Owen Glendower, was quite often seen in the 1920's but he appears to have become quiet of late for there have been no reported sightings of this huge man dressed in a leather jerkin for a number of years.

Cromarty, Rosshire, Scotland

This part of Scotland contains a haunted wood and moor where dozens of ghosts have been seen. Among them are said to be phantoms of warriors in armour engaged in fierce hand to hand combat.

Crossgate, Durham

Here was fought the battle of Neville's Cross on 17th October 1346. According to witnesses the ghost in this area is that of a woman said to be looking for her husband who was killed during the battle. All who have seen her agree that she appears to be desperately trying to get a lift to the battlesite.

Dunphail Castle, Nairnshire, Scotland

Here Scottish folklore says there was a famous siege. The Earl of Moray was besieging the castle and the situation was desperate for the defenders. With food running low Alastair Cummings and a few brave companions escaped the blockading force and stealing some bags of meal threw them over the wall to feed their starving friends. Unfortunately these brave men were caught in the act and promptly beheaded. The severed heads were then thrown over the walls with the famous cry "Here's beef for your bannocks!" The noise of fighting is said to still be heard both within and without the walls of this castle. The severed heads of Alastair and his companions are also claimed to appear from time to time within the castle.

Dunstanburgh Castle, Northumbria

This castle has two known ghosts. The first is Queen Margaret, the wife of King Henry VI, and one of the Lancastrian leaders during the Wars of the Roses. The second ghost is Thomas Earl of Lancaster who was beheaded by order of King Edward II after leading a rebellion against his monarch. This ghost is said to be of horrifying appearance having a blood spattered shirt and a ragged and torn neck. His head is carried in the traditional manner, i.e. under his arm and his face is much contorted with the agony of death.

Dunwhich, Suffolk

Here we have a lost town which was, in the Middle Ages, one of the most prosperous ports in England and now lies under the sea. One resident from that time though has refused to leave. An Elizabethan sailor has been seen from time to time wandering down to the coast before getting in a boat and vanishing.

East Stoke, Nottinghamshire

The ghosts of several naked and semi naked men have been seen here. Tradition relates that these were mercenaries fighting during the Wars of the Roses, who were captured, stripped, humiliated and then killed for their pains.

Fenny Bridges, Devon

Here, in 1549, a very one sided battle took place between rebel peasants and an army loyal to the crown. The Peasants who were part of the Prayer Book Rebellion were massacred, and local tradition has it that if you stand on the bridge on moonless nights you can seen the ghosts of cavalry wading through blood up to the horses hocks.

Flodden Field, Northumbria

At this battle the Scots suffered their greatest ever military defeat. In one bloody afternoon they lost their king as well as the flower of their chivalry, plus of course countless thousands of ordinary men. Instead of sounds of battle or the sighting of a lonely warrior there is a singular ghostly phenomenon. Visitors to the site have reported the appearance of brightly coloured pieces of cloth flapping on the gorse, which fade and vanish from view when they are approached.

Glenlivet, Moray, Scotland

Here in 1594 rebel soldiers were met by a force of troops loyal to King James VI. One of the royalist soldiers was a young man called MacAllister. He was killed by the first cannon shot of the battle which neatly took his head off. His headless spirit has been seen riding around the fields from that day forth.

Hall Place, Bexley, Kent

This was the former home of Edward, the Black Prince, eldest son of King Edward III. It was from this place that he set out in 1347 to fight for his father in France. His ghost is said to return to the hall, clad in his famous armour, and accompanied by ghostly medieval music. His spirit was seen three times during World War II, each time prior to a major setback. As a result he is regarded as a symbol of national misfortune.

Hedgeley Moor, Northumbria

These fields saw, on 25th April 1464, a battle which resulted in another Percy death. This time it was fought during the Wars of the Roses and Sir Ralph Percy, a leading Lancastrian noble, was caught with his host by a larger Royalist army and heavily defeated. Ever since then, the ghost of his horse has been seen riding across the Moor towards what would have been the Yorkist lines. Legend has it that Sir Ralph seeing the hopelessness of the situation rode ahead of his troops towards the Yorkists seeking his own glorious death.

Hermitage Castle, Roxburghshire, Scotland

Among the ghosts sighted in this castle are several soldiers in blood stained armour. These phantoms have been seen within the castle precinct both during the day and night.

Holy Trinity Church, Goodramgate, York

The ghost of Sir Thomas Percy, the 7th Earl of Northumberland has been seen wandering around the churchyard. He was executed by order of Queen Elizabeth I after leading a rebellion against her. It is said that his ghost is eternally searching for his missing head amongst the tombs.

Kidwelly Castle, Carmarthenshire, Wales

A young female warrior called Gwenllian was said to have been beheaded in a battle with the Normans and rode around the countryside for years afterwards looking for her head. When the two parts were finally reunited the haunting stopped, but more recently there have been reports of a medieval soldier seen at this site.

Knaresborough, Yorkshire

Witnesses in the 19th century reported seeing a small unit of soldiers dressed in white tabards, carrying swords and commanded by a man dressed in red. Who they were or what they are doing in the middle of a forest is not known and the sightings have not re-occurred.

Knighton Gorges, Isle of Wight

Here another knight in armour has been seen. This time, though, it is a black knight on horseback who is said to appear every year on 31st December.

Leap Hill, Northumbria

The sounds of a skirmish fought long ago can still be heard here. One of the casualties of that battle was Sir Thomas Ellesden who was decapitated in the fight. His headless ghost has been seen walking in the area of his death, most recently in 1987. Northumbria must truly be called the land of battles for there does not seem to be one acre in that county that has not seen blood spilt on it.

Lewes, Sussex

The battle here was fought on 14th May 1264 between rebel forces lead by Sir Simon de Montfort and a smaller royalist army led by King Henry III and his son Edward. The rebels won the day, capturing the king and later the prince, and for a year the kingdom of England was governed by a parliament of nobles. This event is still reportedly heard in the fields outside the town, the exact day varies.

Lud's Church, Cheshire

The ghost of Alice, a Lollard, who was killed during a raid to break up a meeting of this illegal sect haunts the local chasm, supposedly over the spot where she was buried.

Lustleigh, Devon

A woman riding her horse in the middle years of the 20th century reported sighting a group of horsemen in early medieval costumes coming towards her. It is thought that what she saw were the spirits of a 13th century boundary commission who had been ordered to determine the extent and limits of the forest boundary.

Maddington Manor, Wiltshire

This appears to have a very similar haunting to the previous one. This time the figure is an unknown knight in armour who walks from the building to the churchyard.

Market Bosworth, Leicestershire

Near here was fought the Battle of Bosworth Field on 22nd August 1485, where Richard III lost his life and Henry Tudor took the crown to become King Henry VII. In the nearby town the headless ghost of a man in armour has been seen wandering the lanes looking for his missing head.

Middleham Castle, Yorkshire

This was the birthplace of King Richard III, and is said to be haunted by the sounds of battle coming from outside the castle walls. Three children who reported hearing the sounds also said that they saw a knight on horseback, who charged, causing them to flee.

Mitford Castle, Northumbria

Here there is a particularly terrifying spirit. Two boys who sighted the ghost in 1934 described the figure as a warrior wielding a large sword in one hand and a decapitated head in the other. The fact that the boys fled in terror is not surprising especially when they revealed that they heard a scream, not from the warrior but from the decapitated head.

Neville Castle, Kirkbymoorside

Here the sounds of a battle can occasionally be heard and is said to be the noises of a Scottish army engaging an English one.

Newcastle Cathedral, Newcastle

Here the ghost of a medieval warrior is said to walk through the cathedral although confirmed sightings of this spirit are rare. On one occasion a man examining a crusader's tomb was startled by the noise of clanking behind him, and turned, just in time to see a man in armour disappear around a nearby pillar. He followed the apparition but when he reached the pillar there was of course no further sign of the knight. Puzzled by what he had seen he walked towards the nearby Verger, who was in the company of three elderly ladies, in order to question him about what he had seen. Before he could do so though, all the people present were startled by the noise of what they later described as a heavy body being thrown to the floor. None of the witnesses were able to account for this mysterious sound.

Newcastle, Newcastle

This once fine castle, now sadly mostly destroyed by Victorian railway engineers is haunted by the ghosts of several Norman soldiers. What they make of the trains flying past every day is anyone's guess.

Otterburn, Northumberland

This was more of a border skirmish, between the lords Percy and Douglas, than a pitched battle, and though the Scots claimed the victory their leader, The Earl of Douglas, was killed. These events were played out to witnesses in a taxi going home late one night. Suddenly the engine died and the group found themselves eerily hemmed in by spirits on all sides. To their enormous relief, though, this crowd of phantoms quickly dissipated back into the Northumbrian mists.

Paper Hall, Bradford

Here a pedestrian walking past the entrance to the hall was astonished to see the ghost of a man in shining white armour holding a spear in one hand and happily swaying to and fro whistling a merry tune. This contented spirit has only been seen once.

Pengersick Castle, Cornwall

The spirit of a knight wearing a white tabard with a red cross emblazoned on it has been seen. It is not known if this phantom is also responsible for the footsteps which are often heard late at night in one of the main bedrooms.

Pevensey Castle, Sussex

This castle boasts a ghostly army which has been heard fighting in the area of the ruins. Occasionally the force is also seen marching across the marshes from the sea towards the castle and disappearing in the moat. The exact period to which this army belongs is open to dispute. Some sources claim that the army dates from the reign of William Rufus, the son of William the Conqueror, who unsuccessfully besieged the castle for six days. Other sources, though, claim that he army dates from the reign of Richard II, who is also known to have laid siege to this place.

Peveril Castle, Derbyshire

This site has a phantom knight who has been seen standing by the keep and on the ramparts. His horse is also said to trot around the keep. The banging and clanking noises which have been heard in the castle are also attributed to this knight.

Pistol Meadow, The Lizard Coastline, Cornwall

This area contains the graves of several hundred men who drowned when their ship went down sometime in the 16th century. At least one of those killed has been seen wandering about the field where he is buried.

Pitchford Hall, Somerset

What sets the phantom seen here apart is that his armour is a green colour.

Prudhoe Castle, Northumbria

This site is said to be haunted by the spirit of an unknown knight in full armour.

Ruthin Castle, Clwyd, Wales

This is also haunted by a knight in armour who interestingly only wears one gauntlet. Who he is and, why he is underdressed, is not known.

Ruthven Barracks, Strathspey, Scotland

These ruins date from the Hanoverian period and were built to prevent Jacobite risings in Scotland during the 18th century. However it is not a ghost from this time that haunts the site but one from a much earlier period. The reason for this anomaly is that the barracks were built on the site of a castle belonging to Alexander Stewart, a vicious man better known as the Wolf of Badenoch. It is his ghost that has been seen wandering through the ruins, most often on stormy nights.

Saint Briavel's Castle, Forest of Dean

This now a hotel and is haunted by a figure in full armour that is also heard walking about the hotel both during the night and the day.

Salisbury Hall, St Albans

Like other medieval sites described so far, this hall has the ghost of a knight haunting it. The spirit appears to favour the vicinity of the medieval drawbridge, though, like other sites, who he is or why he appears is not known.

Scarborough Castle, Yorkshire

This site also has the ghost of a man who played for the highest stakes and lost. Piers Gaveston the favourite of King

Edward II was widely hated by the nobles of England eventually being forced to flee the court. In 1312 he was captured at this castle by rebels tired of Edward's mismanagement and executed. His spirit is said to haunt these ruins and has been seen several times, though not recently.

Senlac Hill, Hastings

Here was fought the Battle of Hastings in 1066 between Duke William of Normandy and King Harold Godwinson. It is said that on the anniversary of the battle a knight on horseback appears on the battlefield, some six miles from Hastings. Other figures are known to appear on the site but these are seen much more sporadically.

Shaw Green Lane, Prestbury

This lane is haunted by the ghost of a messenger killed by the Lancastrians during the Wars of the Roses. His manner of death is uncertain for the tradition varies. Some say that he was shot by an arrow, whilst others claim that he was decapitated by a thin wire stretched across the road. However he died, it appears that the man is still trying to get his message through.

St Albans, Herefordshire

In some parts of this town, in particular around Battlefield House, the noises of battle are heard once a year. Here during the Wars of the Roses two vicious battles were fought in the streets of the town in 1455 and 1461.

St Mary the Virgin, Kemsing, Kent

This fine church is haunted, according to tradition, by the spirit of one of the four knights who murdered St Thomas a Becket. On 29th December, the anniversary of Becket's death, this tormented soul is said to gallop up to the building, tether his horse, enter and kneel at the altar praying for a while before disappearing.

St Nicholas' Church, Brighton

A knight on horseback is said to haunt this church, though, why he should do so is unclear.

Stamford Bridge, Yorkshire

This small town also saw a brutal military contest between the armies of King Harold Godwinson and King Harald Hadrada in 1066. The Anglo – Saxons won the fight and slaughtered many of the Vikings, indeed the Viking army needed only 24 ships out of an initial fleet of three hundred to take them back home to Denmark. The battle was fought on 25th September and is said that on some anniversaries the fight is re-enacted in the skies over the town.

The Black Bear Inn, Tewkesbury

This inn is haunted by the ghost of a man in armour who, tradition tells us, was a Lancastrian soldier executed nearby.

The Chough Hotel, Chard, Somerset

Another hotel with the ghostly spirit of a knight in armour. Some say this spirit is linked to the tombstone which can be seen standing behind one of the fireplaces. Furthermore it is said that the stone is impossible to photograph well.

The Fire Brigade Headquarters, Bristol

This modern building is haunted by the ghost of a man that appeared nine times to startled witnesses in 1975. One man thought the ghost was wearing waterproof clothing, but others likened his costume to those worn by the Knight's Templar an organisation which once owned large tracts of land in and around the city.

The Globe, Ludlow

This building is within sight of the Norman castle and is built in the oldest section of the town. The spirit here is said to be Edward Dobsod or Dobson a soldier who was murdered whilst garrisoning Ludlow in either 1513 or 1553. The spirit is described as being average height with a wig and a cloak over one shoulder.

The New Forest

Tradition has it that the ghost of King William Rufus, the son of William the Conqueror walks in the area where he was so mysteriously killed on 2nd August 1100.

Tower Field, Flamborough Castle

This also has a phantom guard. He was last seen a few years ago by a local man who identified him as a Norman soldier carrying a spear over one shoulder.

Weare Gifford Hall, Devon

Two ghosts are said to haunt this site. The first is a voice which shouts "Get you gone!" at terrified visitors. The second is the spirit of Sir Walter Giffard who died in 1243. His ghost is said to walk from the gatehouse of the hall to the neighbouring church in search of his wife.

Ye Olde Trip to Jerusalem, Nottingham

This is said to be Britain's oldest pub and is haunted by the ghost of a Norman knight on horseback. The ghost is always seen in one of the caves dug into the back of the pub which were used in the medieval period as stables.

The 17th Century

It would be no exaggeration to suggest that the 17th century was the most traumatic century in British History. During this period we saw the unification of the crowns of Scotland and England, the rise of the power of parliament, an end to the idea of absolute monarchy and the trial and execution of a rightfully anointed King. The English Civil War, more correctly called, in my opinion, The British Wars of Religion, still holds the dubious record of the bloodiest war in British history given the number killed per head of population. That combined with the witch hunts carried out by characters like Matthew Hopkins, which saw hundreds of innocent men and women killed; the great plague of 1665; and of course the Great Fire of London in 1666, meant that it was a time of fear and distress for many people. This fear appears to have imprinted itself on the British landscape for I came across more military ghosts for this century than I did for any other period of British history.

The English Civil War is officially dated as 1642 – 1645. But the truth is that it started in the late 1630's with Charles I's attempt to force a unified prayer book on all the disparate parts of his realm and doesn't end until the restoration of the monarchy in 1660. During this time families were torn apart as people sided with the King or with Parliament and battles were fought with a ferocity rarely seen in British history. Truly is it said that the 17th century was the century of battles. The Cavaliers and the Roundheads battled to decide the future of Britain and in dong so left an immense ghostly legacy.

A Farm, North Devon

In the 1970's the owner of this farm became so attached to the ghostly Cavalier who would regularly walk through the rooms towards the back of her farmhouse that she went so far as to leave a chair out for him in case he ever felt the need to sit down.

Blacksmiths Forge Tea Rooms, Pluckley, Kent

This is haunted by the ghost of a smiling Cavalier whose jovial spirit wanders around the upstairs rooms and has been seen by several members of the family run business.

Buckstones, Yorkshire

A policeman returning home after a late night shift was startled to see in his headlights a small group of Royalist horsemen riding down the road. Braver than most he then drove past them three times to make sure that they were not a figment of his imagination.

Buttsbury, Essex

Here also is a Cavalier ghost who is most often encountered on the Stock to Ingatestone Road. As with so many others spirits from this time why he haunts this particular spot is not known.

Carlisle, Cumbria

On a more pleasant note, tourists investigating the west wall of this city might well encounter the ghost of a Cavalier dressed in white. He most often appears early in the morning and vanishes before he reaches the wall. The spirit is particularly popular with the people of the city mainly because he is reputed to smile sweetly at any who see him.

Cassiobury, Hertfordshire

This is the ancient home of the Earls of Essex, one of the senior Parliamentary families of the Civil War. Here the ghost of Lord Capel is said to walk on the anniversary of his death. He started off as a Parliamentarian but soon found that their tastes were too austere for him and switched to the Royalist cause. For this he was executed on 9th March 1649.

Castle Coch, Cardiff

Here the spirit of a former owner, who legend says buried his treasure somewhere in the castle before going off to fight for his king, is said to walk at night. According to tradition the unfortunate man was killed when he stood too close to an exploding cannon. This spirit so terrified two retainers in the castle that they at once handed in their notice and gave up their homes in the castle.

Chatwall and Church Stretton, Shropshire

Both of these villages have the ghosts of Cavaliers on horseback. In the first instance the identity of the ghost is not known though he is most often seen riding around the lanes leading into Chatwall. In the second instance the identity of the ghost is known. Major Smalman was a loyal servant of King Charles and as a result his house was besieged by Parliamentary troops in 1645. Despite the success of the siege Smalman was able to escape on horseback and his ghost has been seen on many occasions both in his house and galloping away from it.

Chingle Hall, Longridge

A site we have already encountered twice in this book, also has a ghostly Cavalier to go along with a Roman centurion and a medieval knight.

Christ Church College, Oxford

This was used by King Charles I as his headquarters during the Civil War, as London, which had declared for Parliament, was forbidden to him. Because of this the college is home to two ghosts. The first is that of the king who appears both with and without his head wandering in the grounds of the college. The second is that of a Royalist officer who was supposedly shot for treason on the site.

Dover Castle, Kent

Staff working at the castle have told of sightings of several ghosts from this period. The two most commonly encountered are a pikeman and an officer dressed in Royalist uniform.

Edwin's Hall, Woodham Ferrers, Essex

The hall has three known ghosts one of which is said to be a Cavalier who walks all the rooms and corridors of this dwelling.

Gaulden Manor, Somerset

More wounded Cavaliers have been seen here. This time there are three spirits covered in blood which are seen standing in the chapel in front of a series of carved panels. At least one skirmish was fought in the vicinity of this place during the Civil War and so it is highly likely that these are the ghosts of wounded men brought here to have their wounds treated, or perhaps laid out in the chapel after they had died.

Hitchin Priory, Hertfordshire

The Priory is said to house the spirit of a Cavalier called Goring who was wounded in a nearby skirmish, then later captured by Parliamentary soldiers and beheaded whilst his betrothed watched from an upstairs window. His headless ghost is said to return to the priory on the anniversary of his death, 15th June, and ride to the site of a cell in the grounds.

Holland House, London

This magnificent mansion was built in 1606 by Sir Walter Cope and is haunted by the ghost of the Earl of Holland who was executed at the end of the Civil War for his unrepentant loyalty to the King. The building is now a youth hostel and some guests still witness his unique method of manifestation. Before the ghost appears it is said that three drops of blood appear mysteriously near a hidden door. Then as the clock strikes midnight, his ghost, with his head tucked under his arm, appears and walks through the rooms and corridors of the house he once owned.

Hound Tor, Devon

There has been one sighting of a Cavalier made by a motorist driving along the local road to Hedgebarton. The driver was forced to stop suddenly when he saw a man in a Cavalier's uniform walk out from the shadows into the middle of the road and then vanish suddenly.

Middle Clayden, Buckinghamshire

This site is also haunted by the ghost of a known Cavalier. Sir Edmund Verney was appointed the King's standard bearer and fought bravely at the first battle of the English Civil War, Edgehill, in 1642. At some point during the battle Sir Edmund became isolated and was attacked by Parliamentary soldiers. Though the manner of his death is not known, it is recorded that he held so strong a grip on the standard that even in death he would not let it go. In the end his hand had to be hacked off. The royal standard was later recovered by the Royalists with Verney's hand still attached. The ghost of Sir Edmund Verney is said to return to his old house looking for his missing hand.

Newcastle

Like Carlisle, the people of Newcastle are also quite fond of their Cavalier who, it is said, wanders through various parts of the city laughing as he goes. Tradition tells us that he is Sir Roger Weatherley who lead a small band of Royalists for ten months between the siege of Newcastle and Charles' defeat at Naseby in 1645, though what happened to him after that is not clear.

Pencaet Castle, East Lothian, Scotland

The ghost of King Charles is said to haunt one of the bedrooms of this castle

Prestbury, Gloucestershire

Tradition has it that this ghost is a messenger bringing news of the defeat of King Charles II's forces at the Battle of Worcester in 1651 to the royalist commander of the town.

Reindeer Inn, Banbury, Oxfordshire

There must be something about pubs and Cavaliers for here is another one that also has a ghost. This apparition is described as grim faced as he wandered about the maze of rooms and corridors on the upper floor of the pub. However when Banbury council bought the original panelling in the Globe Room of this pub the ghosts silent walking ceased. The panelling was installed in the new civic centre, so, perhaps instead of finding peace this spirit has simply moved locations.

Rock Hall, Northumbria

This hall contains the repentant spirit of a murderer who got away with it. Sir John Selkeld was a Royalist commander who quarrelled bitterly with a neighbour. One day during an argument he stabbed the man in front of scores of witnesses. However he had proved too useful to his monarch and the affair was allowed to be forgotten. Sir John's spirit has walked the Hall from that day onwards.

Salisbury Hall, St Albans

Another fine mansion containing a Civil War ghost. Along with the spirits of a medieval knight and Nell Gwynne, the ghost of a Cavalier has been seen staggering through the crown chamber with a sword through his stomach. His identity is unknown, but this ghost is also blamed for the disembodied footsteps heard, falteringly, climbing the nearby staircase.

The Binns, West Lothian, Scotland

Here the spirit of General Tam Dalziel has been seen both in the house and in the grounds. He was a staunch royalist during the English Civil War and was captured at the Battle of Worcester in 1651, during an attempt to put Charles I's son, also called Charles, on the throne. After escaping from the Tower of London Tam joined the Czar of Russia's army before returning to Britain in 1660. There he rose to command the Scottish forces of King Charles II from 1666 until his death in 1685.

The Crab and Lobster, Sidlesham

Again we have a Cavalier but this time tradition gives him a name. Sir Robert Earnley defended Chichester bravely for the king and managed to escape from the town when it ultimately surrendered to Parliamentary forces. With a few companions he made his way to Sidlesham hoping to find a boatman to take them to France. However they were betrayed to some Parliamentarian cavalry and in the ensuing fight his two nephews were killed and Sir Robert himself mortally wounded. At this point the tradition differs depending on who tells it. Either Sir Robert died fighting just outside the pub, or dying he was carried inside where he breathed his last in the main bar area. Whatever happened to him, his tall ghostly figure, in uniform and wearing a large cloak, has been seen in the pub in the hours before dawn, as well as on the quayside where tradition puts the fight. On one occasion his ghost was seen in the main bar lying in a pool of blood.

The Crown and Raven Hotel, Somerset

This hotel has two ghosts. The first is a young girl who has been nicknamed Eva. The second is an unknown Cavalier.

The Dun Cow, Shrewsbury

Here a Dutch Army Officer was executed for killing a servant of Prince Rupert's and tradition has it the ghost, in full Dutch uniform, walks the pub late at night.

The Old School Cottages, Bromley Cross

On one occasion the ghost of a Cavalier has been seen materialising out of the walls of this building in broad daylight. On another occasion the sound of marching feet close to the cottage so disturbed the owner that he went outside to investigate. Though he could see no-one he distinctly heard a voice shout the words, 'peril' and 'menace'.

The Olde Rock House, Barton on Irewell

This establishment is haunted by a quick witted Cavalier who managed to elude his pursuers. Fleeing from a royalist defeat, this young man donned a farmers smock, and suitably disguised he walked about the area muttering over and over "Now thus," "Now thus," until his pursuers had passed. His muttering ghost has been seen in the area on occasion re-enacting his escape.

The Ring O' Bells, Middleton

Here is another pub which holds a ghostly Cavalier. Again with a sad face he is described as handsome, carrying a sword and dressed in a cloak and lace collar. Unexplained footsteps have also been heard in the cellar of this establishment and the idea that it is the Cavalier causing them was given credence when helmets and weapons from the 17th century were unearthed there, as well as human bones.

The Salmon Inn, Northumbria

Yet another pub which can claim a ghost Cavalier. Tradition has it that when being pursued by Roundheads the Cavalier hid in an old priest's hiding hole. However terrified at the idea of hiding a fugitive the inn keeper let the poor man starve to death rather than risk the Parliamentary forces finding him. Since that day the ghost of the Cavalier has on occasion been seen, but more often heard and sensed in the pub.

The Stork Hotel, Billinge

This was originally built as a jail in 1640 and was used to house Royalist prisoners during the Civil War. Here in one of the underground cellars a Cavalier was murdered and now haunts the hotel. His ghost seems to have been most active in 1972 when one guest caught sight of him going into the gent's toilet. At other times his disembodied footsteps were heard especially during August of that year.

Three Crowns Hotel, Chagford

A Royalist officer, Sir Sydney Godolphin, died on the doorstep of the hotel and his ghost has been seen many times, the last in 1980, standing by the door of the dining room in full uniform.

Who'd Have Thought It, Milton Coombe

This pub is named after the disbelieving exclamation of a previous landlord when told that he would get the licence to sell beer and spirits, not his rival down the road. The ghost sited here is described as a young, sad faced, individual with long chestnut coloured hair. He is most often seen sitting dejectedly at the end of a bed in one of the rooms, but no-one has been able to find out why he haunts this establishment.

The ghosts of Cavaliers have also been seen at **The Roman Walls, Chester**; **Moresby Hall Cumbria**; the road running through **Hassop, Derbyshire**; **Corfe Castle, Dorset** where the phantoms of several royalist soldiers have been encountered; **Borley Lodge, Essex**; **The Mermaid Public House, Colchester**; **East Street, Colchester**; **Treasue Holt, Essex**; **Winter's Armoury, Essex**, **Church Street, Essex**; **The Green Dragon Alehouse, Waltham Abbey** whose spirit only appears at lunchtime; **The King's Head Hotel, Cirencester**; **Littledean Hall, Forest of Dean**; **The Old Court House, Newent**; **The George Tavern, Strand**; **The Fisheries Inn, London**; **19 Dunraven Street, London**; **The A30** south of Hook, where a young girl in a car reported seeing a Cavalier holding a broken sword; **Prior's Court, Callow End**; **Leicester Guildhall**; **The**

County Assembly Rooms, Lincoln; **The Hippo Club, Nottingham**; **The King Charles Parlour Public House, Wells** and finally **Coal Pit Fields, Bedworth**.

The ghosts of Roundheads conversely are much rarer, perhaps because they won. However their spirits are around and indeed include the most famous character from this period, Oliver Cromwell, whose ghost appears at a number of sites.

All Saints Church, Crondall, Berkshire

This church contains the spirits of several soldiers who have been seen around the church, and one who rides up to the church before vanishing through the door.

Attenborough, Nottinghamshire

A Roundhead cavalry unit has been sighted in this area preparing to cross the body of water there.

Bendrose House, Amersham Common, Berkshire

This also claims to have Cromwell's ghost who appears to take delight in waking guests by giving them a small electric shock. Some though have suggested that nylon bed covers are to blame.

Bigg's Cottage, Wash Common

Here, the Earl of Essex, the Parliamentarian general, slept before the battle of Newbury. It is not his spirit that haunts the building though but that of an unknown sentry who keeps watch as vigilantly today as he did over three hundred years ago.

Carbrook Hall Hotel, Sheffield

This was once the home of Colonel John Bright, one of Parliament's ablest soldiers. The ghost, in a Civil War uniform that has been seen on a number of occasions at the hotel is said to be the colonel returning to keep an eye on things.

Chenies Manor, Buckinghamshire

Here the noise of laughter and several thuds have been heard, the owners of the manor blame the sprits of Roundhead soldiers eternally entertaining local girls as they once must have done.

Coach & Horses Public House, Buckland Brewer, Devon

It is rarer for the puritan soldiers of Parliament to haunt inns and taverns though this site does boast one.

Codnor Castle, Derbyshire

The ruin of this castle has the ghost of a rather scruffy looking Roundhead who witnesses describe as looking tired and desperately in need of a shave.

Faringdon, Berkshire

The church here is said to be haunted by the ghost of Sir Robert Pye. He besieged his own father's hall, Faringdon House, and his headless spirit has been seen lurking by the north wall of the nearby church.

Ghost Hill, Murrow, Cambridgeshire

This appropriately named site is an isolated area of fenland and there have been several reported sightings of Cromwell's ghost, though why he should chose to haunt this small, lonely spot is not known.

High Wycombe, Buckinghamshire

This town is haunted by the ghosts of several soldiers from the period, both Roundhead and Cavalier, who have been seen riding through the lanes of the town. A more famous spirit is John Hampden, one of the Parliamentarian instigators of the Civil War, whose ghost has been seen with some of his green coated infantrymen in the fields surrounding the town on moonlit nights.

Howely Hall, Batley, Yorkshire

The ghosts of several soldiers are said to haunt the area.

Huntingdon Castle, Donegal, Ireland

Another Roundhead trying to make his presence known has been seen knocking on the castle door. The story goes that he dressed as a royalist in order to escape from his pursuers but was shot dead by his own side who did not recognise him.

Lake Burwain, Lancashire

Here units of Roundhead cavalry and infantry have been seen looking tired and dejected

Loughton, Essex

In 2000 a young girl reported seeing the top half of a Roundhead soldier on a wooded path near Loughton Hall.

Lyric Bingo Hall, Wellingborough

Another interesting place to find this most stern of puritans is here where a young medium is said to have conversed with Cromwell, whom historians know used the building as a headquarters for a few days during the Civil War.

Pinocchio's Restaurant in Walton le Dale, Lancashire

In 2003 a photograph taken here is said to show the ghost of Cromwell who has long been reputed to haunt this establishment.

Red Lion Square, London

After the restoration of the Monarchy in 1660 the bodies of Oliver Cromwell, his son in law Henry Ireton, and John Bradshaw, who had been the presiding judge at the trial of King Charles I, were all exhumed, put on trial, convicted of treason and hanged, drawn and quartered. The night before the sentence was carried out the bodies of Cromwell and Ireton were kept at the Red Lion Inn which used to stand where the square is today. That according to tradition is why the ghosts of the three regicides are said to appear deep in conversation walking diagonally across the square before gradually disappearing.

St Margaret, East Wellow, Hampshire

The ghost of Colonel William Morton, one of the men who signed Charles I's death warrant is said to haunt the Church.

St Mary's Church, Great Baddow, Essex

This also houses the ghost of a Roundhead and he has been seen by several witnesses standing outside.

Stapleton Woods, Bristol

Here a Roundhead is said to approach people desperately trying to say something. Unnervingly, he then proceeds to walk straight through them.

Stubley Old Hall, Derbyshire

Another Roundhead has been seen here though sightings of this ghost have become rarer of late.

Sydney Sussex College, Cambridge

After his body was quartered Cromwell's head was smuggled from its spike and eventually buried at his old college. Ever since then the frightening spectacle of his floating head has been seen in the main hall.

The A34 bypass at Newbury

At least one mass grave from the battle of Newbury was disturbed when the bypass was constructed. Since then the ghosts of several Civil War soldiers, both Roundhead and Cavalier have been seen by motorists.

The Cross Keys, Saffron Walden, Essex

Here there is rumoured to be a lady phantom that tradition says was a mistress of Oliver Cromwell.

The Golden Lion, St Ives

This was used for a time by Cromwell and his staff as a district headquarters. Room number 13 was Cromwell's room and is now furnished in the style of the period. So haunted was this room that visitors refused to sleep in it. The owners changed the room number to 12 but this has not stopped Cromwell from appearing to several startled guests.

The Old Sun Inn, Saffron Walden, Essex

This inn has a Roundhead ghost described as a particularly noisy fellow, responsible for moving furniture and banging on the walls.

The Rake Inn, Rochdale, Lancashire

A particularly merry looking ghost is said to haunt this inn, so real is he that he has often been mistaken for an actual person.

The Salutation Inn, Nottingham

Has among its known ghosts a rather friendly Roundhead, carrying a firelock who once offered a young boy a bite from his apple. What the boy's response to this kind act was is not recorded. This spirit was last seen in the autumn of 1996 by four witnesses who spent a night at the inn.

The Skirrid Mountain Inn, Abergaveny, Wales

This was former courthouse where it is claimed 182 people were hanged. One of the ghosts seen at the inn is that of a Parliamentarian soldier, though it is not known if he was one of those executed at the site.

The Swan Inn, Romsey, Hampshire

Has the spirits of two tormented Roundheads who were hanged from the sign of the pub. Their ghosts have been heard gasping and crying for help.

Wheston Hall, Derbyshire

This hall has the ghost of a Roundhead soldier whom the owners have nicknamed Dick.

Wig and Pen Club, the Strand, London

Before its burial in Cambridge the head of Cromwell was briefly displayed near here and that is why the headless ghost of Cromwell is said to haunt these premises, though without a head surely it is difficult to pin down the spirit's identity.

I called the 17th century the 'Century of Battles' and it is true that there are more haunted battlesites from this period than there are for any other. It appears that the terror experienced by the soldiers on both sides facing terrible deaths, not just on the battlefield, but also from the wounds suffered has often imprinted itself on the atmosphere.

Alvaston, Derby

The sounds of horses, men shouting and gunfire have been heard in this area. These noises are ascribed to a Civil War battle though there is no record of one being fought at this site.

Arundel, Sussex

The noise of firing cannon has been heard on occasion. This is said to date from the siege of the castle by Sir William Waller who attempted to storm the fortress at least once.

Blickling Hall, Norfolk

Sir Henry Hobart's ghost has been encountered in the south west turret bedroom where he died from his wound following his duel with Oliver le Neve.

Castle Hill, Torrington

The Battle of Torrington was also fought after the end of the Civil War and the town is said to be haunted by the ghost of a soldier who was killed in the fight.

Cheriton, Hampshire

Ghosts of soldiers from this period have been seen at the battlesite.

Duelling Stone at Aylsham

On 21st August 1698 a duel was fought between Sir Henry Hobart and Oliver le Neve. Within minutes it was apparent that Sir Henry was facing not just an opponent of greater skill but also a left hander as well. Oliver quickly wounded Sir Henry and that wound proved fatal. Ever since that day this stone has been haunted by the sound of clashing swords and the groans of the dying Sir Henry.

Edgehill, Vale of the Red Horse, Warwickshire

This is the most famous haunted battlefield of the Civil War and was the first large scale battle to be fought, in 1642. Historians still debate who won the battle, but Charles' army was left with possession of the field at the end of the day and a clear route to London. Just a few months after the battle was fought word reached the King that a phantom re-enactment had been seen of the conflict. Disturbed by the news he sent several eminent men to investigate. They reported back that they themselves had seen the haunting which still occurs to this day. Though the spectacular visual of the battle, seen in the skies above, has faded, the sounds of the fighting can still be heard every 23rd October, the anniversary of the fight.

Grafton Regis, Northamptonshire

On 23rd December 1943, six workers on a building site reported hearing gunfire, charging horses and clashing swords.

Hopton, Shropshire

Here a five week siege took place when 28 Roundheads held the castle against a much larger royalist force. They only surrendered after being promised by the royalist commander that their lives would be spared. This however was a trick and all 28 brave defenders were executed after surrendering the castle. Their ghosts are said to appear every 14th March in the ruins.

Landsdown, Somerset

Horses have also been seen here where a particularly bloody battle was fought.

Lostwithiel, Cornwall

This was the site of a Parliamentary defeat and the noises of galloping horses have been heard.

Maghull, Liverpool

The Civil War did not end completely with the destruction of the King's army at Naseby for rebellions broke out periodically after the King had been captured. One of these rebellions seems to have left a ghost or two behind for parts of the town are said to be haunted by the sounds of fighting. One possibility is that in 1648 this area was involved in a small rebellion against Parliament, but it was quickly crushed, and the sounds date from various skirmishes fought between loyalist troops and rebels. However another possibility has been put forward to account for the noises. Parts of the Jacobite army of 1745 also passed this way and it is not inconceivable that fighting occurred in this area at that time.

Marston Moor, Yorkshire

This was the scene of a major battle in 1644 where the forces of Prince Rupert were heavily defeated and the north of England was lost to the King. The ghosts of men slain in the battle, including soldiers from the Marquis of Newcastle's Whitecoats, who famously refused to surrender and were slaughtered to a man, have been seen by many witnesses. In November 1932 a commercial traveller driving with a friend from Scarborough to Harrogate crossed the moor in poor visibility. Meeting a bus on the road the driver of that vehicle warned the two people that he had seen men crossing the road. A few moments later they saw three men in cloaks, wide brimmed hats and dark boots. By the time the bus had passed them the men had disappeared.

Old Basing House, Hampshire

The final place where the ghost of Oliver Cromwell has been seen. This house famously withstood a three year siege from 1642 – 1645, under the command of its owner the Royalist Marquis of Winchester, during which over 2000 Parliamentary soldiers were killed. The fortifications were finally stormed on 14th October 1645 and the house was taken with much slaughter of its inhabitants. Cromwell's ghost was traditionally said to walk from a barn at Lyckpit across to Plovers Dell though it has not been seen for many years. A more regularly encountered phantom is the ghost of a Cavalier, who has been seen on the nearby Common and was likely one of the house's brave defenders.

Poyntington, Somerset

In 1646, one of the last bands of die hard royalists, lead by a young man called Baldwin Malet, were wiped out in a small skirmish here. Baldwin, being a man of some substance, was buried in the local churchyard whilst his men were buried in a local meadow, where it is still possible to see some of their grave mounds today. It is in this meadow that the ghosts of several headless men have been seen along with the spirit of a young woman who somehow got caught up in the slaughter.

Roundway Hill, Wiltshire

Here, where 800 men were killed in 1643, the ghosts of galloping horses have been seen in particular in the area known as Bloody Ditch.

Sandbach, Cheshire

In 1651 Charles II attempted to take the throne of England but was eventually defeated at the battle of Worcester. Another battle fought in that year was at this site where a small skirmish broke out between Scots, loyal to Charles II and locals. The Scots were heavily beaten and their ghosts are reportedly seen in the area from time to time.

St Lawrence's Church, Alton, Hampshire

At this church the sounds of fighting have been ascribed to a small skirmish where a royalist colonel and his men were trapped by a larger Parliamentary force and all killed.

The Battle of Naseby, Northamptonshire

This battle, fought in 1645 saw the final defeat of the King's army at the hands of Parliaments New Model Army. Defeat spelt the end for the Royalist forces and their remaining centres of resistance quickly crumbled. As at Edgehill the battle is said to be repeated from time to time in the skies above, though the passing of time seems to be affecting this vision as it is now no longer seen as regularly as it was reported one hundred years ago.

The Governor's House, Bridgnorth

This house is said to be haunted by the noises of a horse galloping up to the front door, the door opening, and booted feet running up the staircase. According to tradition this is a re-enactment of an event which happened during the war when a messenger hurried to tell Lady Bridgnorth of the death of her son.

The Kings Manor, York

This fine building is said to be haunted by the cries and groans of wounded men brought here for treatment after the Battle of Marston Moor.

The Olde Starr Inn, York

This site was also used as a makeshift hospital and morgue after the Battle of Marston Moor, and like the King's manor is also haunted by the cries of the wounded soldiers. Also the ghosts of two black cats have been seen at the inn.

Wardour Castle, Wiltshire

The ghost of Lady Arundel is said to haunt this castle which she held, with 25 soldiers, for five days against a much larger Roundhead force.

Winnington Bridge, Northwhich, Cheshire

Naseby was not the last battle of The English Civil War, that honour goes to an action here where a small force of mounted Cavaliers were defeated by an equal number of Roundheads. Though no ghosts have been sighted at the spot, a feeling of panic is said to be felt by some people and this, tradition says, comes from the fleeing Cavaliers.

Woodcroft Manor, Peterborough

The manor is haunted by the sounds of fighting, and the cry of "mercy." These noises are most often heard in the summer time and are said to come from Dr Michael Hudson, one of the King's chaplains and leader of a small band of royalist guerrilla fighters. He and his men were eventually cornered in the Hall and died fighting. Dr Hudson was the last left standing and was eventually driven over the parapet by sheer weight of numbers. He begged his assailants to show mercy but they savagely cut at his fingers until the brave chaplain fell to his death.

Other skirmishes which can still be heard today were fought at **Freezing Hill, Bath** and **Rowton, Cheshire**.

After the death of King Charles II Britain received her first Catholic monarch since the reign of Mary Tudor, over a hundred years earlier, in the person of King James II. This was too much for The Duke of Monmouth, the eldest illegitimate son of the previous king, he landed with a small invasion force but was defeated at the battle of Sedgemoor on 6th July 1685. His army, mostly comprising of peasants from the local regions, was poorly equipped and even more poorly lead and were brutally crushed by the Bloody Assizes after the rebellion collapsed. The defeat and the reprisals have left many spirits trapped in the nearby countryside.

Boldre, Hampshire

This is haunted by the ghost of a young man who was killed in the house for the jewellery he was carrying, his body was then buried in the garden. Tradition goes a little further and says that this man had been one of Monmouth's messengers and was resting overnight at the house after fleeing from the defeat at Sedgemoor.

Marlpitts Hill, Honiton, Devon

Another military ghost sighting from the Battle of Sedgemoor involves a party of schoolchildren out with their teacher for the day who were amazed to see the ghost of a man in a mud covered brown coat stagger past them, though their teacher saw nothing It is thought that they were the last witnesses to the ghost of a man who died just yards from his home after being defeated .

Taunton Castle, Somerset

This was used as a temporary prison for any captured rebels. The sounds of booted footsteps are said to be from these rebels being escorted by government troops, and the ghost of a well dressed young man carrying a sword and pistol from this period has also be seen.

The Heddon Oak, Somerset

This famous oak, some 50 miles from the battle, is also said to be haunted for it was used by government forces as a hanging tree for the rebels. For years the ground around the tree has been haunted by the sounds of running footsteps and galloping hooves, as well as choking and strangulation noises. The last time these sounds manifested themselves to a witness was in 1994.

Westonzoyland, Somerset

This was where the Battle of Sedgemoor was fought and the ghosts of fleeing peasants have been seen, as well as a richly dressed man on horseback, said to be the Duke of Monmouth. During the battle the peasant forces were stopped by the Bussex Rhine, one of the many small streams that littered the area. Tragically this stream, which looked wide, was only a foot or so deep and so could easily have been crossed. No-one volunteered to find out however and so the peasants of Monmouth's army trapped on one side died in their hundreds at the hands of the cannon of King James' army. The cries and screams of the peasants and the shout of "come over here and fight" have also been heard at the battlesite.

In the end the autocratic nature of King James rule was too much and in 1688, William Prince of Orange landed with an army of Dutch, English and German troops and overthrew the last Stuart King.

Ford House, Newton Abbot, Devon

This is supposed to have the ghost of William whose nervous pacing up and down the corridors and rooms of this fine house have been heard since that first anxious night on British soil.

Scotland suffered from as much conflict in the 17th century as England did and many of her castles and fields are haunted as a result.

Duntrune Castle, Argyll, Scotland

Duntrune Castle has the ghost of a piper whom legend says had been sent as a spy by the Irishman Coll Ciotach to reconnoitre the defences of this Campbell castle. Coll is said to have hated the Campbell clan. Realising that an attack on the castle would be suicide the piper succeeded in warning off Coll, and his men, by playing his pipes, even though he knew that such an act would seal his fate. The piper was duly punished by having his fingers cut off and bleeding to death. Since that day the ghostly wail of his pipes have been heard in the Tower Room where he was imprisoned awaiting his fate.

Glencoe, Argyll, Scotland

Known as the 'vale of weeping' in Gaelic. Here on 13th February 1692 the famous massacre took place when thirty two members of the MacDonald clan were slaughtered in their beds by a company of British soldiers lead by Colin Campbell of Glen Lyon. This massacre ordered by the British government was supposed to reinforce governmental control in the unruly highlands. Instead it was remembered as a breaking of the oaths of hospitality and a butchery of old men, women and children. It is said that the shades of those killed return to their former homes, especially on the anniversary.

Inverary Castle

This castle is haunted by a harpist who was hanged by Montrose's men when they took the place in 1644. The sounds of his harp have been heard in many of the rooms of the castle.

Killiecrankie, Perthshire

Here the first battle fought in the Jacobite rebellions took place on 27th July 1689 between the forces of Viscount John Graham of Claverhouse, better known as Bonnie Dundee, who supported the deposed James II, and the loyalist forces of General Hugh Mackay. The Jacobites won the battle but, tragically for their cause, Dundee was killed. Several people have reported seeing ghostly remnants from this battle including one poor woman who, whilst picnicking at the site, suddenly saw the bodies of several dead English officers lying at her feet. Others have reported that the pass takes on a strange red glow on the anniversary of the battle.

Newark Castle, Fife, Scotland

After the defeat of the Marquis of Montrose at the battle of Philiphaugh in 1645 many of his men and camp followers, some of them Irish women, were taken to Newark where they were slaughtered in an orgy of killing. The place where the killing occurred is said to be haunted by the ghostly screams of those so brutally butchered.

Pitreavie Castle, Dunfermline, Fife, Scotland

Tradition says that this site is haunted by the ghost of a headless highlander who was killed at the nearby battle of Pitreavie in 1651.

It is not just in Scotland that the ghosts of Scottish soldiers from this period have been seen for many of them were to die in battles in England both for and against the King. In 1650 the Scots came out in support of King Charles II but were heavily defeated by Cromwell at the Battle of Dunbar.

Alnwick Castle, Northumbria

Some of the Scottish soldiers taken prisoner in the battle were force marched to this place and many died through brutal treatment or lack of provisions. The ghostly wails heard on occasion in the castle grounds are said to belong either to these men or to their womenfolk bewailing their fate after walking the road from Dunbar to Alnwick.

Hermitage Green Lane, Newton le willows, Lancashire

The sounds of marching feet have been heard. They are said to originate from the execution of a group of Scottish loyalists in 1650 and are the sounds of the men being marched to their execution. These noises were last heard in January 1990 when the sound of drumming accompanied it, though the witnesses could see nothing.

St Nicholas' Cathedral, Newcastle

The cathedral is haunted by the noises of men in pain. During the Civil War the Cathedral was used to house captured Scottish prisoners some of whom were wounded. It appears that these souls are unwilling to leave their place of imprisonment.

The 18th & 19th Centuries

These two centuries saw Britain's rise from a prosperous country to the world's leading economic and military power. In doing so Britain had to see off two old enemies. The first, in the 18th century, the Jacobites and their desire to return the Stuart dynasty to the throne, and the second, in the 19th century, the militaristic power of the French under Napoleon. Britain's victories over these two enemies helped to establish the British Empire, which grew to be the largest ever seen in history. It is possibly because so many of her soldiers died in foreign fields that there are few military ghosts from these centuries haunting Britain itself.

In 1715 and 1745 there were military campaigns in Britain to re-establish Stuart absolute monarchy. These Jacobite rebellions, though ultimately failing, helped in the militarisation of Britain and a strengthening of Parliament's power. The 1715 rebellion had the best chance of success as it had wide Tory support, however James, the Old Pretender, was not a man to inspire confidence, and his commander the Earl of Mar was militarily inept, as a result the rebellion spectacularly collapsed. Not before leaving a ghost or two behind though.

Dilston, Northumberland

Some joined the 1715 rebellion because they were ordered to by their lords, some joined because they felt it was the right thing to do, the Earl of Derwentwater joined because he was nagged constantly by his wife. The owner of this fine mansion was one of the few lords of England to be executed for joining the rebellion and his ghost along with some of the men he took with him are said to ride around the moors at night. In August 1986, a young woman driving to see her family in Hexham saw the earl in her rear view mirror riding across the road behind her. The ghost of the earl's wife is said to haunt the hall eternally wringing her hands with grief at the memory of the man she sent to his death.

Eilean Donan Castle, Loch Duich, Highlands, Scotland

The Jacobites tried again in 1719, this time with Spanish, not French, support. However this rebellion collapsed even more spectacularly than in 1715. After the defeat of the rebel forces at the Battle of Glenshiel the guns of the government troops were turned on the castle which a small force of Spanish soldiers had managed to occupy. After a brief bombardment which wrecked the castle, the Spanish surrendered but not before at least one of them had been killed. It is his ghost that has been seen in various rooms of the rebuilt castle.

Moresby Hall, Whitehaven, Cumbria

The owner of this hall had strong Jacobite sympathies, so when a young supporter fleeing the collapse of the rebellion called on him for shelter, the man was only to happy to oblige. Unfortunately the soldier was hidden too well and when the owner was summoned to London to explain himself before Parliament he forgot to tell his servants. As a result the young Jacobite starved to death in one of the hidden rooms of the hall. His body has never been found, but his ghost has been seen in some of the rooms and corridors of the hall.

The 1745 rebellion was the most successful rebellion given that the rebel troops managed to reach as far south as Derby before they turned back to Scotland and their eventual defeat on the moors at Culloden. They appear to have left at least three ghosts in England from their famous march not to mention others that are left behind in Scotland.

Culloden House, Invernesshire, Scotland

Some of Bonnie Prince Charlie's troops were brought to the house after the Battle of Culloden many of whom were either dead or dying. For this reason the ghost seen here, dressed in a grey tartan plaid, is said by some to be not Bonnie Prince Charlie but one of the many unknown men who died instead.

Loch Morar, Mallaig, Scotland

After the defeat of the rebellion one of its supporters, Simon Fraser, Lord Lovat hid on one of the islands in the loch until he was eventually captured by government soldiers. His ghost has been seen on the island and was described by one witness as a small fat man suffering badly from gout.

Maghull, Liverpool

This is possibly haunted by a Jacobite ghost, though, as I said earlier, the nationality of this ghost is open to dispute.

Old Parsonage, Handforth, Cheshire

Here the ghost of Bonnie Prince Charlie has been seen and his ghost is said to have so scared a woman that she dropped dead. Her ghost has also been seen in the house.

The Battle of Culloden, Invernesshire, Scotland

Fought on 16th April 1746, this was the last battle to occur on British soil and saw the shattering of the Jacobite dream. Here on this lonely boggy moor the tired, hungry and dispirited Jacobites charged unconvincingly at the ordered ranks of the government soldiers and were slaughtered. This most melancholy of battlesites is haunted by the ghost of a young highland man who has been seen wandering the site as well as lying on top of one of the burial cairns.

The County Hotel, Dumfries

Here Charlie has been seen again, the last time in 1936.

The Rovers Return Trinket Shop, Shudehill, Manchester

This is said to be haunted by the ghost of a young Jacobite soldier who has been seen gazing at a picture of Bonnie Prince Charlie and Flora MacDonald. Mr Francis Shaw, who witnessed the phantom, described him as being of medium height and build with auburn hair and carrying a dirk.

The Jacobite Rebellions of 1715, 1719 and 1745 are not the only incidents to have left ghosts behind. Other sites with spirits from this century include:

Great Pulteney Street, Bath

Admiral Howe, once lived in a house along this street and his phantom has been encountered there late at night.

Inverawe House, Argyll, Scotland

Here the spirit of Duncan Campbell, who was killed at the battle of Ticonderoga, Canada in 1758, has been seen in various rooms of the house.

St Georges Park, York

Finally we come to the sad death of the Earl of Stafford who fought an unknown opponent in a duel here, but within seconds it was apparent that he was outclassed and soon was killed. His ghost has been seen in the Park and is said to wander up to people before disappearing. The ghostly duel has also been witnessed by some people who thought they were seeing a real event until the scene mysteriously vanished before their eyes.

The Queen Anne Block, Royal Naval College

The ghost of Admiral John Byng, who was executed for neglect of duty, haunts some of the rooms here, where he was confined prior to his execution. His shimmering apparition has often been seen, most recently on 15th June 1993, when a security guard saw him walk up a flight of stairs at 11 pm.

As I said at the beginning of this chapter the 19th century was dominated, militarily speaking, by the Napoleonic Wars which culminated in the battle of Waterloo in 1815. This series of European wide wars and coalitions saw Britain emerge as the leading seapower of the age with a rapidly expanding empire as well.

Alma Lane, Crondall, Hampshire

Here the ghost is reputed to be an orderly returning to Aldershot with the news of victory at Waterloo. He was unfortunately waylaid and murdered by highwaymen and his running footsteps have been heard down the lane ever since.

Castlemilk, Glasgow, Scotland

The ghost of a man has been seen riding up to the entrance before disappearing. Tradition says that it is the ghost of Captain William Stirling Stuart who is for ever repeating his return from the battlefield of Waterloo.

Dover Castle

Dover Castle is said to be haunted by the ghost of a drummer boy who was murdered in the castle at the beginning of the 19th century and whose drumming has disturbed the sleep of many visitors and guests, as well as serving soldiers.

Duns Castle, Borders, Scotland

The castle is haunted by the ghost of Alexander Hay who died at the Battle of Waterloo. He has been seen in full uniform in several rooms of the castle.

Grenadier Pub, London

During the early 1800's the pub was used as a mess for officers of the Duke of Wellington's Regiment. One day during a game of cards, one of the officers was caught cheating and viciously flogged by his fellow players. So terrible was the beating that the young man died after staggering to the steps leading to the cellar. Every September, the month in which the man died, the pub is home to a variety of paranormal incidents including objects moving, tables and chairs rattling and footsteps and moans heard in empty rooms. On one occasion a Chief Superintendent from New Scotland Yard saw wisps of smoke emanating from around him. He reached out towards the source of the smoke only to feel a sharp pain as if he had touched the end of a lit cigarette.

Pentland Manor House, London

The ghost haunting this site is reputed to be Robert Smith who was killed in a naval engagement.

The TSW Studio's, Plymouth

The studio site is said to be haunted by a variety of Napoleonic period ghosts whose graves were disturbed when the building was constructed. It is these ghosts who have been blamed for the variety of phenomena that have occurred in the building, which include voices, footsteps and objects being moved.

During the Napoleonic Wars thousands of French prisoners were taken in both naval and land engagements. Many of those were kept in Britain in appalling conditions in old prisons, or prison hulks, the rotting remnants of ships the navy no longer used. Some of those taken were extradited back home both during and after the war, but others did not survive their treatment and their ghosts can be encountered in many of the places used to house them.

Dartmoor Prison, Devon

This must have been a lonely place for the French held there, their ghosts have been both seen and heard in the shell of this former prison. Some of those who did not survive were buried in the prison burial ground, and their ghosts are said to be seen there at night, probably because their graves have been disturbed on a number of occasions.

Dovercourt, Essex

The area is said to be haunted by numerous spirits of French prisoners who were killed when the jetty they were building collapsed on them.

The Birdcage Inn, Thame, Oxfordshire

This is another pub with a disputed phantom. The ghost manifests itself as footsteps in the night and is either a leper who was stoned to death in the area of the inn in the Middle Ages, or a French POW who was once held in the pub's cellar.

The Chequers, Smarden

This is a fourteenth century pub with a Napoleonic ghost. However his identity is open to question. Some say that he was a British soldier murdered on his return from the war for the fat purse he carried. Others, though say, that the ghost is of a French prisoner who was killed after escaping from nearby Sissinghurst Castle, used at the time as a detention centre for French prisoners. Perhaps the ghostly noises of footsteps pacing up and down is more the action of a nervous escapee, than a relaxed ex soldier returning home.

The Royal British Legion, Brixham

This has a French POW ghost who can be seen sitting at the bar and has been nicknamed Francois by the regulars.

One of the heroes of the Napoleonic Wars was Admiral Lord Nelson, whose victories at the Nile, Copenhagen and Trafalgar guaranteed Britain's dominance of the sea and ensured her coasts were safe from invasion. His ghost has been seen in several places.

Brewer Street, London

On a morbid note Nelson's ghost has on occasion been seen looking in the window of a particular shop on this street. According to tradition on the eve of his departure in 1805 Nelson visited an undertaker here and ordered a coffin for himself, perhaps he had a premonition of his imminent death at the Battle of Trafalgar.

Dawlish, Devon

Lord Nelson and Lady Hamilton's ghosts are said to walk along the seafront here and have been sighted several times in the early hours of the morning.

Somerset House, London

This old Admiralty building also claims Nelson's spirit. During the Napoleonic period the house was originally used to house offices of the Admiralty. As a result Nelson was a frequent visitor to the establishment and came to the place for the final time in 1805 to receive his orders to pursue and attack the combined Franco Spanish fleet. This he managed to do at the Battle of Trafalgar which famously saw him mortal wounded on the quarterdeck of his flagship HMS Victory. On bright summer mornings his ghost has been seen skipping across the uneven flagstones of the courtyard, with a wispy semi transparent cloud hovering over his head.

The Gun Tavern, London

Finally this was where tradition says that Nelson and Lady Hamilton used to conduct clandestine meetings and they are said to haunt this tavern late at night.

Other phantoms from the 19th century have been reported from a variety of other locations including:

Ballindalloch Castle, Banffshire, Scotland

The ghost of General James Grant has haunted his old home since his death in 1806. His spirit is said to ride around the castle every night on a white horse and has also been seen in the castle especially in a corridor at the base of one of the towers.

Balmuto, Fife, Scotland

Another Scottish castle with a ghost, this is where the spirit of Sir Alexander Boswell is supposed to walk. He was killed in a duel at the place on 26th March 1822 fighting against a descendant of the Earl of Moray.

Dunnose Point, The Isle of Wight

Here on 24th March 1878 the training ship HMS Eurydice sank after being caught in a violent storm. The ghost of the ship is said to reappear off the point from time to time. A film crew filming in the area with Prince Edward in 1998 may have caught the ship on film, though the image is unclear.

Feering Church, Essex

Another young son to die on a foreign field in the 19th century was John Hardman who was killed in the Zulu Wars. His ghost covered in blood with his hands holding a stomach wound has been seen here. This spirit was most often seen in the last few years of the 19th century but has been quiet of late.

Fort George, Invernesshire, Scotland

This fortified barracks was built after the 1745 rebellion in order to ensure the security of the northern regions of Britain. It is still a working barracks and is haunted by the ghost of a young soldier who hanged himself in the 19th century. His spirit nicknamed Abernethy has been seen in the camp jail and the medical centre, where the suicide took place.

The Angel Hotel, Guildford

Where the ghost of a Polish officer has been seen and was sketched by a female guest in 1970, at 3 o' clock in the morning, when he appeared in her mirror. Why an officer of Polish origin should haunt this hotel is unknown.

The Imphal Barracks, Fulford, York

These barracks are said to be haunted by the ghost of a soldier in a late 19th century uniform. Who he is tradition does not say but in 1969 he so scared a young soldier that the man had to spend several days in the sick bay.

Wheel Cottage, Thundersley, Essex

A former owner of this house tragically lost two of her sons in the Crimean War. Desperate to contact them again she turned to spiritualism and often would blow a trumpet to try and summon their spirits. It is unclear whether the trumpet blasts heard in the cottage at night are from her, or from her sons responding.

The First World War

The Great War saw the deaths of nearly one million serving British and Empire troops between 1914 and 1918. Men were sniped at, mowed down by machine gun fire, blown apart by artillery, gassed, suffocated in badly ventilated dug outs, crushed when those dugouts collapsed, executed by their own side, run over by trucks and even kicked to death by horses. It is no wonder that the trauma suffered by those who survived and the sense of loss experienced by so many families has left a vivid legacy on the haunting of Britain.

Balcombe Railway Tunnel, Sussex

The ghosts of three, or four, First World War soldiers, depending on the source, have been seen in the tunnel. The story goes that they were killed by a train whilst sheltering from a storm.

Bodelwyddan Castle, Bodelwyddan, Wales

This castle was used as a temporary hospital during the First World War to cope with the massive influx of wounded men from the front. The ghost of one of those men is still said to wander the rooms along with a host of other phantoms, including a Victorian woman and a shadowy figure.

Bournemouth Town Hall, Dorset

Once a year it is said that the ghost of a soldier appears at the public fountain here to help himself to a drink of water though his identity and the date of his appearances is unknown.

Cloud's Hill, Bovington, Dorset

In 1925 this house was bought by T E Lawrence, better known as Lawrence of Arabia. He truly loved the building and once promised never to leave it. This promise appears to have come true. Ten years after buying the house Lawrence was killed in a nearby lane on his motorcycle. Visitors to the cottage have reported sighting his spirit in a white Arabic costume as well as hearing the sound of a Brough Superior motorcycle, the type that Lawrence was riding when he died, coming towards them in the early hours of the morning.

Fulwood Barracks, Preston

These barracks are haunted by the ghost of a chaplain who was killed in France and returned to his base. His ghost has been seen leaning against his sword whilst at other times witnesses have heard heavy breathing and clapping, which is ascribed to the same spirit.

Golden Hill Fort, Isle of Wight

This site claims two spirits, the first is that of a sailor from an unknown period who has been seen regularly and appears to enjoy watching people work. The other, and much more rarely seen, is a First World War soldier whose identity is unknown.

Hayling Avenue, Portsmouth

This was the site of one of those paranormal events which rarely reoccur but which baffle when they do happen. A woman walking down the lane passed a detachment of First

World War soldiers walking past her in the opposite direction. Noticing their uniform styles she quickly looked behind her only to find that the men had vanished.

Hendon RAF Museum, London

A number of paranormal phenomena have occurred in this museum, including the sounds of footsteps, engine cowls being lifted and engines running. The sounds are ascribed to Flight Lieutenant Shepherd who died in a plane crash in 1917.

Holy Trinity Churchyard, Wingate, Durham

This cemetery is haunted by a most unusual manifestation. On some nights the gravestone marking the burial of Corporal Longstaff, who was killed in action in 1918, has been seen glowing eerily.

Ickelsahm Village Pond, Surrey

The ghost of a First World War soldier has been seen gliding across this pond. The best viewpoint is from the car park of the Robin Hood Public House.

RAF Upavon, Wiltshire

A First World War pilot has been seen in full flying gear at this airfield. Though his identity is unknown it is said that he crashed his plane on a moonlit night in a field nearby.

Rothiemay Castle, Aberdeenshire, Scotland

This Castle is haunted by a ghost from the early part of the war. Lieutenant Colonel J Foster Forbes was killed in one of the first battles of the BEF in 1914 and his uniformed ghost is said to return to his old family home from time to time.

The Black Swan Public House, Bow Road, London

One of the many Zeppelin raids carried out against London in the First World War destroyed this pub with a direct hit by a bomb. Ever since, the ghosts of those patrons killed are said to return from time to time to continue their drinking and their games.

The Coliseum, St Martin's Lane, London

For a short while this building was haunted by the ghost of a soldier who spent his last night of leave here before returning to the front and his death. The ghost would walk down the gangway and turn into the second row of the dress circle and then vanish, just as the lights were dimming.

The Langham Hotel, London

Here the ghost of a German soldier has been seen in some of the rooms. According to tradition he was visiting this country on the eve of the war, depressed by his countries desire for the coming conflict he committed suicide by jumping from one of the windows.

The Lyric Theatre, Shaftesbury Avenue, London

Another victim of a Zeppelin raid is said to haunt this theatre. The figure of an usherette, killed by a bomb dropped by one of Count Zeppelin's creations, has been seen walking down the aisles of the theatre just as she must have done in real life.

The Old Vicarage, Grantchester

One of the most popular poets at the start of the war was Rupert Brookes who died on active service in 1915. His ghost is reputed to walk his old house where disembodied footsteps are heard walking around the outside of the house and in the sitting room. His spirit has also been seen in the garden and poltergeist activity, reported on the top floor, where books are often moved from the shelves.

The Theatre Royal, Winchester, Hampshire

One of the former lighting operators at this theatre went off to fight on the western front and never returned. His ghost, dressed in combat clothing, has been seen in the backstage areas. The ghost of a former owner of the theatre, Mr John Simpkins, has also been seen in the building.

The Tomb of the Unknown Soldier, Westminster Abbey, London

This is as poignant a place as you can find in Britain. Here on 11th November 1920 the complete, though unidentified body, of a British soldier was buried in soil gathered from all the battlefields of France beneath a marble stone quarried in Belgium. Occasionally, when the crowds of tourists have dispersed, the ghost of a soldier materialises by the tomb and stares at it in a posture of mourning, for a few minutes.

The White Swan Pub, Newbury

Another pilot from the Great War has been seen on the roads bordering this pub. On one occasion two people stopped to give him a lift only to find him disappear in the back of their car. When they reached the pub they explained what had happened and were given the distinct impression that this had happened before, though the locals were unwilling to go into any detail.

Between the Wars

There have been a few reported sightings of ghosts that are dated between 1918 and 1939 and these are covered in this brief chapter.

Buckingham Palace, London

One of the ghosts said to haunt the Queen's primary residence is the spirit of Major John Gwynne. He was involved in a divorce scandal and snubbed by polite society. Ashamed of what had happened he retired one night to his first floor office room and shot himself. Since that event cleaners and staff in the room have reported being overwhelmed by feelings of depression, as well as occasionally hearing a noise similar to a gun being fired.

St Alban's Church, Fulwood Barracks, Preston

This church is haunted by the uniformed ghost of a soldier said to have been killed in Ireland in the early 1920's. His spirit has most often been seen standing near the lectern which was taken from a church in Ballincolig in County Cork and set up in this church on 25th June 1922. The same ghost is also said to be responsible for the sounds of heavy breathing and clapping occasionally heard at this site.

Windsor Castle, London

In 1927 a young guardsman commited suicide in the Long Walk area of the castle. His ghost has been seen and heard pacing out his watch just as he did all those years ago.

The Second World War

At 11.15 am on Sunday September 3rd 1939, Prime Minister Neville Chamberlain announced to the British people, in grave tones, that Britain was again at war with Germany. The failure of politicians after the First World War to realise that humiliating Germany would lead to a rise in nationalistic fervour, something that Hitler so ably tapped into, and thus a return to global conflict, meant that just 21 years after 'the war to end wars' the world was plunged once more into war. This time the devastation would be truly terrible. Britain would suffer the deaths of 377 000 serving soldiers and around 70 000 civilians. The effects of this last great war are still felt today and the terror and hurt experienced by so many ordinary people has imprinted itself on both the psyche and the psychic of the people and places of Britain.

The first battle ever fought solely in the air occurred over the skies of Britain when the 'few' of the Royal Air Force faced the Luftwaffe in the Battle of Britain during the summer of 1940. This battle has left an immense legacy of hauntings both in the buildings and the airfields used by those young men of the RAF.

Burscough Airfield, Lancashire

This site has now been given over to farmland. Farmers working here have reported being approached by an RAF officer smoking a pipe, who bids them a warm 'good evening' before disappearing.

Burtonwood Old Airfield, Cambridgeshire

An airman who was decapitated when he attempted to bail out of a burning aircraft has been seen in this area.

Cambridge Airport, Cambridgeshire

This is an old airbase that has been modernised and several witnesses have reported sighting phantom pilots in RAF gear. Auditory noises have also been heard including the sounds of footsteps and on one occasion ghostly singing.

Croydon Aerodrome, London

This former airfield has now been heavily built on but the ghosts of the past still remain. In 1940 during the initial stages of the Battle of Britain the Luftwaffe successfully bombed many RAF stations. This one was badly hit and 72 people were killed. The ghostly voices occasionally heard in the area are said to come from those who died during the air raid. In 1971 a witness reported seeing a RAF officer on a motorcycle travelling at high speed. Strangely this phantom, which has been reported by other people, has no face. Others have reported seeing pilots from the war walking around the remnants of the runways, now built over.

East Cowes, Isle of Wight

Here the eerie spirit of a headless airman parachuting down to earth has been seen. A security officer and his dog once saw this phantom and it so terrified the animal that it later had to be put down.

Holmsley South Airfield, Hampshire

Here the ghosts are auditory not visible. The sounds of planes taking off, and music from the 1940's, has been heard across this desolate airfield.

Imperial War Museum, Duxford, Cambridgeshire

The control tower of this former base is haunted by the ghost of an American crew who hit the building whilst attempting to land. Other people have heard the sounds of a low flying aircraft and hanger 5 is supposed to be full of paranormal activity though what has been witnessed is unclear.

Lakenheath Airforce Base, Suffolk

An RAF pilot has been encountered a number of times in the main road leading to this base, and on one occasion was even given a lift by an USAAF policeman. Another ghost has been seen walking across one of the runways, usually on bright moonlit nights, and is said to be the spirit of an Australian pilot who died when his bomber crashed.

Langham Apple Orchard, Norfolk

This was a former USAAF airbase and some of those pilots have been seen amongst the trees here. The sound of a crashing aircraft has also been seen, as has screaming which reportedly was heard once from the end of the former runway.

Montrose Aerodrome, Angus, Scotland

This claims to be the most haunted airfield in Britain and it is true that a variety of paranormal phenomena have occurred here. The sounds of flying aircraft coming into land are frequently reported. In 1987 a woman driving in the vicinity of the airfield reported sighting a Hawker Hurricane in the air, when she enquired at the local Museum Society about any historic aircraft she was informed that none were flying that day though during the war a number of planes had crashed at the airfield including at least one Hurricane fighter. On other occasions the sounds of footsteps have disturbed witnesses as has the ghost of an airman encountered on the runway. Twice in 1990 ad 1991 people were scared off the runway by a shadowy creature, possibly the same one seen by the son of the museum curator in 1994.

North Pickenham, Norfolk

Another former airbase where the sounds of an aircraft warming up prior to take off have been heard in the remains of one of the wartime hangars.

North Weald Airbase, Essex

This site had a number of phantoms of which only one appears to be active today. A WAAF who died in a bombing raid was seen in the area where she was killed for about twelve years after her death. During the war a badly wounded airman was taken inside the control tower where he succumbed to his wounds. His body was found cradling the telephone and it appears he died trying to make a call, though to whom is not known. For years afterwards his ghost was blamed for interfering with the telephone and on occasion removing it from its holder. The ghost who is still seen on site is that of an airman who it is said was pinned to a tree and killed by an explosion.

Parham Airfield, Suffolk

Locals living nearby this disused airbase have reported hearing aircraft in the skies whilst the control tower was haunted by phantom wet footprints which began and ended mysteriously.

RAF Bassingbourne, Cambridgeshire

This was a base used by the USAAF during the war and is supposed to be haunted by the ghosts of phantom crews. These were most often sighted in the 1960's though they have been quiet of late.

RAF Biggin Hill, Kent

One of the main fighter stations during the Battle of Britain this airfield is haunted by the sounds of a Merlin engine which has been heard usually in the late afternoon. Occasionally the ghost of a spitfire has accompanied it. World War II airmen dressed in greatcoats have also been seen in the nearby village asking directions to the airfield.

RAF Binbrook, Lincolnshire

This former airfield is said to have a haunted bomb dump and the ghosts of several pilots, though it is not known if these phantoms are linked to one incident or not.

RAF Bircham Newton

The ghost of a friendly pilot, who is often seen laughing, haunts this site along with a WAAF (Woman's Auxiliary Air Force) who is supposed to have committed suicide, as well the sounds of footsteps which follow any witnesses.

RAF Bottesford, Leicestershire

This is a well preserved example of an RAF station from the war period and a variety of paranormal incidents have been reported. A ghost bomber has been seen flying over the airbase on a number of occasions, usually at dusk. Noises and flashing lights have been seen and heard in the old control tower, and finally the ghost of an airman has been encountered on the main runway.

RAF Bourn, East Anglia

Two female witnesses walking back to their digs at the teacher training college at Bedford heard music coming from one of the empty Nissan huts still standing in this former airfield. As they stood listening for a while the music stopped and the sounds of men laughing were heard.

RAF Colbey Grange, Lincolnshire

The ruin of the watchtower overlooking the runway of this airfield is haunted by the sounds of a watch tower in action. An RAF officer has also been seen in the vicinity. Tradition says that he is a remorseful ghost who regrets sending so many young men to their deaths in the skies over Britain.

RAF Cosford, Shropshire

Not so much a haunted airfield as a haunted bomber, an Avro Lincoln to be exact. The first time it was seen was in 1977 when a witness, carrying out repairs on the machine, saw him sitting on a toolbox. Ever since then the spirit has been reported by a number of people and has been seen both inside and outside the bomber, which is reported to be very warm inside even on cold days. On other occasions ghostly footsteps have been heard as well as a catchy but unidentified tune being whistled. Witnesses have also reported hearing the sounds of a bomber in service around the plane, engines running, crew's voices and Morse code. Others have seen ghostly crew members in the plane itself. On one occasion a film crew near the bomber scoffed at the idea of ghosts only to have one of their cameras thrown across the hangar. Needless to say they did not scoff any more after that.

RAF Digby, Lincolnshire

This is an airfield that is still in use by the RAF, was first commissioned in the First World War. There have been a number of sightings of an RAF officer on a bicycle who stops startled passers by and asks for the keys to the watchtower. This building is also haunted by the sounds of people speaking and a mysterious light which flashes on and off.

RAF Driffield, Yorkshire

A young airman forced to bail out of his aircraft, over this base, landed safely on the control tower. Unfortunately he died falling from this building to the ground. His ghost has been seen from time to time descending slowly towards the control tower.

RAF East Kirkby, Lincolnshire

In 1944 a USAAF pilot crashed and died near the site. His ghost has been seen dragging his parachute behind him, walking along the old runway. A pilot thought to be the same spirit has also been seen in the old watch tower.

RAF Fiskerton, Lincolnshire

The control tower of this former airfield was said to be haunted by the ghostly voices of men trying to get in contact with a lost bomber. Sadly these voices can no longer be heard as the watchtower was demolished several years ago. However the ghost of an RAF officer has been encountered several times on-site and one witness reported sighting a jeep full of airmen driving past him at high speed, only to disappear.

RAF Grove, Oxfordshire

This site has now been converted into office blocks and in one of them the ghost of a pilot in full flying gear, including oxygen mask, has been seen.

RAF Hawkinge, Kent

This site now houses the Kent Battle of Britain Museum and visitors have reported hearing the sounds of planes ready to take off; the ghost of an airman who walks as if injured; and a noise similar to a V1 rocket.

RAF Hemswell, Lincolnshire

This is another former airfield which is haunted by the sounds of the past. In 1978 a man driving home stopped here for a rest and distinctly heard music which he identified as The Missouri Waltz, a tune popular during the Second World War. As the music stopped he heard an engine starting up, a lorry stopping and people speaking and laughing. Unable to see anything to account for what he was hearing the man quickly got back into his car and drove away. Other sources suggest that two other phantoms have been seen here. The first is a pilot who has been seen on the runway with his clothes on fire, and the second is a mechanic whose arm was torn off in an accident and whose ghost has been seen staggering around the site screaming.

RAF Kelstern, Lincolnshire

The noise of a Merlin engine has also been heard overhead at this ruined airfield, whilst nearby the ghost of a pilot has been seen trying to hitch a lift to the abandoned airbase.

RAF Kimbolton, Huntingdon, Cambridgeshire

This was used by the USAF as a bomber base and the ghosts of several American airmen have been seen. Tradition has it that they belong to the same crew who crashed their bomber in a field nearby.

RAF Kirton – in – Linsey, Lincolnshire

This former RAF site is now occupied by the army. Soldiers have reported a number of strange incidents. A pilot has been encountered in a number of places, and the sound of a terrifying scream has been heard. During the Battle of Britain barrack block 37, which housed a number of free French pilots, suffered a direct hit and many were klled. Ever since witnesses have reported hearing garbled conversations in French coming from the area of that building.

RAF Leconfield, Beverley, Yorkshire

The ghost of an airman has been seen in the traffic control tower here. The last witness to see the ghost reported only being able to see the bottom half of his body as the top half was obscured by machinery.

RAF Leeming, Yorkshire

After the war this airfield was upgraded in order to cope with modern aeroplanes. During the process several workers on the site reported paranormal activities. One man returning from a fishing trip nearby reported hearing the sounds of men's voices and saw the figure of an airman sitting on a low wall nearby. He put his fishing gear down to approach the man only to see him disappear when he stood up. This figure had also been seen by one of the cooks on site. He later confided that he and his wife had moved out of their on-site accommodation after seeing the ghosts of several airman playing cards, and hearing the voices of men in the night. Later investigations revealed that a poacher who often crossed the airfield at night had seen, on several occasions, the ghosts of men walking into a nearby mound which, tradition says, contains the buried wreckage of a crashed bomber.

RAF Lichfield, Staffordshire

The ghost of an aircraft gunner has been seen here. This decapitated spirit is said to originate with an incident when a man committed suicide by deliberately walking into the spinning propeller of a Wellington bomber. The site is now an industrial complex and a number of workers have reported seeing this phantom, as well as another one, this time with a head. On other occasions security guards walking their beat have reported that their guard dogs refused to enter certain parts of the complex.

RAF Lindholme, Yorkshire

Here the ghosts of two individuals have been sighted. The first is known as 'The Jigsaw Ghost' and originates from an incident early in the war when a mechanic took a Wellington Bomber up and crashed it whilst attempting to land, he himself dying in the incident. When helpers found his body it had been torn in two by the force of the impact and held together only by his flying suit. The ensuing ghost, which has been seen on a number of occasions, moves in an odd way as if his legs were separate from his body, hence the name. The second spirit is said to be the ghost of a Polish pilot who crashed his bomber into a bog near the airfield. His crew died in the crash but he managed to stagger into the officer's mess before falling down dead. His phantom, nicknamed Lindholme Billy, has been seen in various parts of the airfield and reports are that he asks directions to either the sick quarters or the operations room. The story of the crashed bomber was give credence in the 1970's when the bog was drained and a wrecked bomber was found with some of the crew still inside.

RAF Manby, Lincolnshire

The main ghost most often encountered on this site is of an armourer who committed suicide during the war. He has been seen often near the armoury wearing his uniform, a greatcoat and gumboots. Other incidents include a ghostly tramp, the sounds of an aircraft and the mysterious movement of a caravan with three people in it in the middle of the night.

RAF Mepel, Cambridgeshire

An RAF pilot has been sighted in the area of this airfield and on one occasion an RAF police officer encountered the spirit only to be told to not bother reporting it as the ghost had been so often seen. Others in the area have reported hearing the sounds of a phantom aircraft.

RAF Northolt, London

The ghost of a pilot in full flying gear has been seen walking along the eastern runway.

RAF Rufforth, Yorkshire

During the Second World War one bomber crashed spectacularly on this site, which resulted not only in the wrecked plane but also a destroyed farmhouse, and three other damaged bombers, as well as more tragically a dozen deaths. The ghostly crew responsible for the devastation have been sited in the ruins of one of the hangars at this site.

RAF Sawbridgeworth, Hertfordshire

An airman has been seen sitting on the side of the road leading to this former airbase. Tradition has it that he is waiting for a lift. If that is true, he has been waiting a long time.

RAF Scampton, Lincolnshire

The ghost of a pilot has been seen at this site and is thought to be responsible for the disembodied 'hello' which once greeted a visitor to one of the deserted hangars. The voices of men chatting have also been heard in the crew room.

RAF Strubby, Lincolnshire

The spirit of a headless airman, killed when his plane crashed during a night flying exercise, has been seen here. On one occasion an airman was hospitalised after sighting the ghost.

RAF Waltham, Lincolnshire

Waltham airfield was taken over after the war and used by a variety of companies who retained some of the old wartime buildings. It is in these that the ghosts of several airman of the time have been seen. One witness saw a pilot walk through a hangar wall where he was working. In 1969 a girl sleeping in a house built on part of the old airfield saw a young man in an RAF uniform with ginger hair and one sleeve pinned to his chest. Her screams woke her parents though they arrived too late to see the ghost who had quickly vanished. A memorial to those airmen from this airfield killed during the war stands on the site of one of the former runways and here, usually around dusk, the ghost of a pilot has been seen.

RAF Welford, Berkshire

The crew of a Lancaster bomber which crashed shortly after taking off, due to being overloaded, has been seen walking across the old runway. Furthermore this was one of the last places that Glen Miller stayed before his fateful airplane trip in which he died. The Glen Miller hangar, where the band leader played, is said to be an eerie place to visit at night, and even the local wildlife avoid the building. As yet though no paranormal activity has been encountered there.

RAF Wellesbourne Mountford, Warwickshire

Here the ghost of a navigator has been encountered, always near one of the main hangars. The story goes that he was killed when he ran into a spinning propeller.

RAF West Malling, Kent

The ghost of a pilot in flying kit is often seen here and it is said that several of the preserved Second World War buildings have an unpleasant atmosphere. In 1981 the site was being used by a film crew and the director had to ask if the two airmen and a WAAF who were looking into the engine of a jeep could move out of the shot. One of the film crew approached them only to have the whole scene vanish in front of everyone. The sound of a Merlin engine has also been reported by people who live near the former airfield.

RAF Whitchurch, Bristol

The ghost of a Luftwaffe pilot is said to haunt the remains of the airfield and has been seen by various witnesses. Presumably he crashed his plane in the area, though no records have yet been found to prove this.

RAF Wickenby, Lincolnshire

This was the former home of the famous 626 squadron and is said to be haunted by the ghost of a WAAF who committed suicide after hearing of the death of her boyfriend. A one off ghost was encountered during the war by Michael Bentine, who later found fame in The Goon Show. Walking towards his hut he passed an old friend whom he greeted. His friend, known as Pop, nodded in acknowledgement and walked by. Later he discovered that 'Pop' had been killed two days earlier.

RAF Wittering, Cambridgeshire

Another control tower hit by a crashing bomber is situated here. The scene is supposed to be re enacted on occasion. Either a ghostly bomber slowly descends to earth only to disappear before contact with the ground is made, or the bomber actually hits the watch tower. Phantom airmen have also been scene in the vicinity where the bomber disappears and lights and noises have been encountered in the tower.

Ridgewell Airfield, Essex

This field is haunted by the sounds of airplanes crashing and shouting voices

Stretton, Cheshire

This was the site of a naval air station and was said to be haunted by a young man who had been killed when he accidentally walked into a propeller. This ghost was most often seen in the two decades following the Second World War, but has been quiet of late.

Teeside Airport, County Durham

The identity of the ghost seen here is open to dispute, but what is not in dispute is that the two candidates are both heroes. The first is a Polish pilot officer Mynarski, who was awarded a posthumous Victoria Cross for his attempts to free a trapped rear gunner from their plummeting bomber. Mynarski died in the attempt whilst the rear gunner was blown clear when the aircraft exploded in mid air. The other possible identity of the ghost is that of a Canadian pilot who ordered his men to bale out but stayed at the controls, to make sure the bomber did not hit Darlington, and died in the crash. Whoever the ghost is he is most often encountered in the corridors of the Teeside Airport Hotel as well as in the wartime hangars.

Turweston Airfield, Northamptonshire

The ghost of a pilot has been seen here on occasion. In 1950 a duty cook encountered the spirit when he entered one of the billets. The ghost disappeared when the man cried out in astonishment.

Washington Airport, Sunderland

Here the ghost of a Second World War pilot has been seen sometimes hovering a foot off the ground. He is described as a tall young man with blue eyes and a small moustache, wearing full flying kit with an oxygen mask dangling down to his waist.

The ghosts of pilots and their planes from the Second World War have not just been encountered in their former airfields; indeed they have a habit of turning up in the most peculiar of places.

Abbey Road & Tavy Bridge, Thamesmead, Kent

During the war at least one known plane crashed in this area, and the pilot of the unlucky Spitfire has been seen in a number of the buildings that flank this road. Other witnesses have also reported the sounds of a German plane crashing here.

Addington, London

A German pilot has been seen walking in this area, and has haunted the site since his plane crashed here early in the war.

B1052, Hadstock, Essex

The ghost of an American pilot has been seen trying to hitchhike on this road. Tradition has it he was killed in a plane crash and is trying to get back to his airbase.

Bethnal Green Tube Station, London

One of the worst tragedies that took place during the Blitz occurred here. The protected station received a direct hit by a German bomb killing one hundred and seventy three people, including many women and children. Late at night the sounds of children crying and women screaming have been reported by the station masters.

Church Broughton, Derbyshire

A Second World War Bomber moving silently has been seen in the skies above this town.

Cirencester, Gloucestershire

The ghost of a young USAAF pilot has been seen standing next to the Queen Anne's column in the park. He appears to be trying to speak to people but disappears after attempting a single sentence.

Colwyn Bay, Wales

Whilst on holiday in this area a family watched a silent Second World War bomber fly inland and disappear behind a hill.

Coventry Cathedral, Coventry

The city suffered heavily in one particular German attack and its medieval cathedral was destroyed. Since then several people wandering about the ruins have heard the sounds of phantom planes flying overhead.

Disused Sand Pit, Clacton – on – Sea, Essex

Three German pilots have been seen loitering in this area, the last time by a group of children. It is believed that they are the crew of an ME 110 which crashed close by. The site is currently a car park and the crew have not been seen now for a few years.

Garrowby Hill, Stamford Bridge, Yorkshire

A female witness reported a most unusual apparition here in August 1999. Apparently a young man in an RAF uniform walked up to her introduced himself as John and then vanished just as she was about to shake his hand. Who this ghost is, and why he haunts this site, will probably remain a mystery.

Hengrove Park, Bristol

The ghost of an airman who was killed in a plane crash here is said to wander the park trying to figure out where he is.

Hope, Derbyshire

Mr Tony Ingle watched a silent aircraft fly past him some forty feet above the ground and dive behind a hill. He rushed to the area expecting to see the wreckage of a plane crash, only to find no crash site and no sign of the plane.

Lamport, Northamptonshire

The road leading to this abandoned air force base is supposed to be haunted by a ghostly car full of young airman which slowly fades from view.

Longendale Valley, Derbyshire

In 1997 dozens of people were astonished to see an aircraft crash in this valley. Many of them called the emergency services but a search of the area failed to find anything. Two planes are known to have crashed here, a B29 bomber, at the end of World War Two, and an F13 transporter in 1946. Of the two the bomber is the more favoured candidate and the captain of this aircraft is said to haunt the area where his plane went down.

M11 Southbound, Woodford, Essex

This ghost has not been seen since the road was altered. Before that, however, the ghost of a German pilot would often be seen on the hard shoulder. One witness reported seeing him six times.

Ripe Lane, Ripe, Surrey

This lane, bordering on a field near the village, is supposed to be haunted by the ghost of a German pilot whose plane crashed here during the war.

Rolls Royce Factory, Bankfield, Barnoldswick, Lancashire

In January 2004 there were repeated sightings of a Lancaster Bomber flying over the factory, throughout the month. In all some thirty witnesses claimed to have sighted the craft.

Saddleworth Moor, Rishworth, Lancashire

On 15th August 1995 a man and his daughter spotted a bomber flying nearby with smoke pouring out of its left engine. As they passed under a bridge the aircraft disappeared.

Tangmere Aviation Museum, Surrey

This former RAF base was heavily bombed during the early part of the Battle of Britain. During one raid several WAAF's were killed and their screaming voices have occasionally been heard late at night after the museum has closed.

The Capricorn Club, Brightstone, Isle of Wight

This site suffered a direct hit during a German bombing raid and one of its victims, an unknown officer, has haunted the bar area ever since.

The Eagle Hotel, King's Lynn, Norfolk

In June 1942 this building was destroyed in a German air raid. It was rebuilt in the fifties though some of the victims of that raid survived into the new build. Various owners of the building have reported the sounds of a party late at night in full swing.

The Golden Fleece Public House, York

Towards the end of the Second World War a Canadian pilot, who had been celebrating a little too much with his comrades, fell to his death from an upstairs window. Ever since his uniformed ghost has haunted the room from which he fell.

The King's Arms, Peckham Rye, London

This pub was hit by a bomb in 1940, during the blitz, and totally destroyed. The bodies of eleven people were dragged out of the rubble and is it supposed to be their spirits which haunt the new building. The sounds of singing have been heard, accompanied by a phantom piano, and the ghost of a woman in a 1940's dress has been seen from time to time.

The King's Head Public House, Cullompton, Devon

In a fight in this pub during the war a USAAF airman was stabbed to death and his ghost, in uniform, has been seen in the main bar area.

The Leather Exchange Public House, Leathermarket Street, London

So terrible were the casualties suffered during the Blitz that many places were converted into temporary morgues to cope with the number of the dead. The cellars of this pub was one such place and it is said that the spirits of those killed have remained behind, though actual details are vague.

The Naval and Military Club, Picadilly, London

Another victim of the Blitz is said to haunt this site. The spirit of Major Henry Bradell has been encountered by many witnesses as it walks through the club, smiling.

The Petwood Hotel, Woodhal Spa, Lincolnshire

This was the former mess of 617 squadron, the famous 'Dambusters' and the spirits of some of their pilots appear to have been left behind. Noises like a party in full swing as well as voices and footsteps have been heard at night when the hotel was empty.

The River View Park Estate, Gravesend, Kent

The ghost of a German pilot, whose plane was shot down in this area, is supposed to haunt this housing estate.

The Towy Valley, Dyfed, Wales

Here a phantom Wellington Bomber which flies in complete silence at tree top level along the valley has been reported by a number of witnesses.

Woodbridge Bar, Woodbridge, Suffolk

This site is supposed to be haunted by the ghosts of several ex-airmen, along with the phantom of an old woman dressed in a night shirt.

The ghosts from other branches of Britain's military services are also said to haunt some of the buildings and regions of Britain, though not in the same quantity as with the RAF.

Bovington Tank Museum, Dorset

The phantom of a German panzer officer has been seen here staring at a Tiger Tank whom, according to tradition, he commanded and was killed in during the war.

Conington Railway Junction, Cambridgeshire

There is disagreement as to the identity of the ghost seen here. Some say that it is the phantom of a German POW who died in a lorry crash here. Others, though, point to death of Colonel Mellows who died in 1948 when his car was hit by a train, as a more likely source for the ghost.

Dover Castle, Kent

Beneath the medieval castle are miles of tunnels and underground rooms used during the war for a variety of command purposes. Guided tours through these various sites have encountered a variety of paranormal incidents. On one occasion a man and his daughter had a conversation with a ghost who told them that his name was Bill Billings and that he had been a Telecommunications Officer who had been killed in an accident attempting to assemble an amplifier rack. Searches through the available records of the time failed to turn up any information on the man, though it has to be said that the records are not complete for the war period. Other ghosts seen here include a man in a naval uniform.

Fauld Crater, Hanbury, Staffordshire

One of the largest explosions to occur during the Second World War happened here when an ammunition dump exploded, killing many people and utterly destroying several farm buildings. The sounds of people crying have been heard in the vicinity of the crater as well as a voice shouting right at the point of detonation.

McPhersons Paintworks, Bury

This site of this paintworks was, according to tradition, used as a POW camp for Germans during the war. One former inmate, who supposedly hanged himself, has been encountered by various staff members, including a security guard and his dog. Cleaners have reported being tapped on their shoulders and having lights mysteriously flick on and off.

North Deans, Lowestoft

The ghost of a uniformed man has been seen at the nearby sea defences pointing out to sea. The last time this spirit was encountered was in 2006.

The Castle of Mey, Caithness, Scotland

This was the home of the late Queen Mother. There have been reported sightings of several phantoms here including the ghost of a Black Watch Piper who was shot dead at his post during the war, though the reasons behind his shooting remain a mystery.

The Channel Islands

These were the only parts of Great Britain to be occupied by the German Army. Because of this there have been many sightings of German soldiers in houses where they were billeted on the islands during the war. Other Germans on bicycles have also been seen on the roads leading to the old airport. Visitors to the gun emplacements at Les Rouvets and La Vasselerie have encountered terrible feelings of panic and distress whilst in the ruins.

The Goat Inn, Strumpshaw, Norfolk

A previous landlord of the inn reported seeing phantom figures and the sounds of a piano. According to some, these events are caused by the ghost of a sailor who drowned when his ship went down during the war.

Unknown Ghosts

This last chapter is devoted to those ghosts that I could not place in any of the historical periods covered in this work.

Aberdeen, Grampian, Scotland

The site of the former barracks in King Street is haunted by the ghost of an officer from the Gordon Highlanders. Tradition has it that he lost his nerve after being told his unit was to be shipped overseas, and committed suicide.

Bestwood Lodge, Nottinghamshire

This building was formerly a barracks and is said to be haunted by the ghostly sounds of an injured soldier in great pain.

Cadover Bridge, Dartmoor

Here the sounds of a small battle have been heard, though from what date is unknown.

Clacton – on – Sea

Near where the old Martello tower used to stand the ghost of a soldier killed in a fight has been seen. This area has undergone heavy redevelopment and the sprit has not been seen since.

College Green, Bristol

This area contains the angry spirit of an executed soldier who was killed for deserting on the eve of battle.

Donnington Castle, Berkshire

The ghost of a soldier standing guard at the gatehouse of this castle has been seen along with a white dog that appears also to haunt the hill on which the castle stands.

Glen Shiel, Highlands, Scotland

No doubt the site of many a clan battle this beautiful part of Scotland is said to be haunted by the ghosts of fighting men armed with swords and muskets.

Gun Hill, Southwold

Said to have been killed when a cannon exploded and decapitated him, the ghost of a naval gunner has been seen standing by some of the old guns here.

Hooten Lane, Leigh

Here sometime in the past a soldier drowned in a nearby pond and his ghost has been encountered deliberately creeping up on passers by to terrify them.

Inverary, Argyll and Bute, Scotland

Dressed in their red uniforms this unit of phantom English soldiers is said to march in perfect formation along the A819 out of town.

Mill Hill Barracks, London

This site is claimed to be haunted by the sounds of footsteps said to come from the ghost of a young soldier who committed suicide here sometime in the past.

Moat Farm, Downham Market, Norfolk

During the late 19th century it was claimed that this site was often enveloped in an eerie mist and that the sounds of a battle could be heard. This interesting phenomena has not been encountered for nearly a hundred years and it is likely that whatever caused the reports has since disappeared.

Morwenna Park Estate, Northam

Almost as soon as this housing estate was built there came reports of residents sighting ghosts. One child reported seeing soldiers in the vicinity of his house whilst another saw a tall black cloaked figure; children's imagination? Possibly.

Newhouse Inn, Dartmoor

Here the spirit of a military man in a grey cloak has been seen riding in the vicinity of the ruins of this former inn.

South Efford House, Aveton Gifford

A particularly foul mouthed spirit haunts this site. It is said to be a naval officer, who has been heard shouting and swearing at night in deserted rooms.

The Falstaff Public House, Derby

It is claimed that four spirits reside in this pub including the shade of a sergeant major. His identity and the reason for this haunting is unknown.

The High Street, Holme Hale, Norfolk

Two witnesses reported hearing fighting at this site as well. The noises appeared to run through the village and into a nearby field before ceasing.

The Naval Dockyard, Plymouth

Over one hundred sailors are known to have been hanged here for various crimes and their ghosts are still said to pervade the atmosphere of the hanging site.

The Old Mitre Inn, Farnham

An unknown soldier is said to haunt the front entrance of this inn dressed in a bright uniform.

The Schooner Hotel, Alnmouth

This site is claimed to be the most haunted hotel in the country. Among its many ghosts is that of a soldier, though like so many others why he should chose to haunt this site is unknown.

Windmill House, Bishop's Stortford

The grounds around this house are said to be haunted by the ghost of a soldier who was accidentally killed here.

Bibliography

Brooks J A: *Ghosts of London*, Jarrold Publishing, 1993

Brooks J A: *Ghosts and Legends of the Lake District*, Jarrold Colour Publications, 1988

Brooks J A: *Ghosts and Legends of Wales*, Jarrold Publishing, 1987

Brown T: *Devon Ghosts*, Jarrold Publishing, 1982

Campbell M: *Strange Tales of Perthshire*, Lang Syne Publishers LTD, 1990

Cohen D: *Encyclopaedia of Ghosts*, Guild Publishing London, 1984

Coventry M: *Haunted Castles and Houses of Scotland*, Goblinshead Musselburgh, 2004

Foley B: *The Ghost Walk of York*, Heslington Publications, 1988

Foreman J: *Haunted Royal Homes*, Jarrold Publishing, 1992

Fry E & Harvey R: *Haunted Gloucester*, Tempus, 2004

Gordon G (ed): *Scottish Ghost Stories*, Lomond Books, 2000

Hallam J: *The Haunted Inns of England*, Wolfe Publishing LTD, 1972

Halpenny B P: *Ghost Stations*, Casdec LTD, 1990

Hillsdon S: *Jersey Witches, Ghosts & Traditions*, Jarrold Colour Publications, 1987

Hippisley Coxe A D: *Haunted Britain*, Hutchinson of London, 1973

Hole C: *Haunted England*, Fitzhouse Books London, 1940

Hough P: *Supernatural Britain A Guide to Britain's Most Haunted Places*, Piatkus, 1995

Jones R: *Walking Haunted London*, New Holland Publishers LTD, 1999

Kristen C: *Ghost Trails of Northumbria*, Casdec LTD, 1992

Kristen C: *More Ghost Trails of Northumbria*, Casdec LTD, 1993

Linahan L: *The North of England Ghost Trial*, Constable and Company LTD, 1997

Ludlam H (ed): *Elliot O'Donnells's Ghost Hunters*, W. Foulsham & Co. LTD, 1971

Matthews R: *Haunted York*, A Pitkin Guide, 1992

McCarthy C: *Some Ghostly Tales of Shropshire*, Shropshire Libraries, 1988

McEwan G J: *Haunted Churches of England*, Robert Hale, 1989

Moss P: *Ghosts Over Britain True Accounts of Modern Hauntings*, Book Club Associates, 1977

Poole K B: *Britain's Haunted Heritage*, Magna Books, 1998

Puttick B: *Ghosts of Buckinghamshire*, Countryside Books, 1995

Queux S L: *Haunted Bristol*, Tempus, 2004

Readers Digest Association LTD: *Folklore, Myths and Legends of Britain*, 1977

Reynolds H: *Ghosts and Legends of Northumbria*, Coquet Editions, 1990

Roberts T: *Myths and Legends of Wales*, Abercastle Publications, 1992

Robinson P & Hesp P: *More Ghosts & Hauntings from the East Riding*, Hutton Press LTD, 1988

Robson A: *Grisly Trails and Ghostly Tales*, Virgin Books, 1992

Sampson C: *Ghosts of the Broads*, Jarrold Colour Publications, 1976

Seafield L: *Scottish Ghosts*, Lomond Books, 2002

Thomas P: *Llanfihangel Legends*, Prontaprint, 1989

Underwood P: *Gazeteer of Scottish and Irish Ghosts*, Souvenir Press, 1973

Underwood P: *Ghosts of North West England*, Fontana/Collins, 1978

Underwood P: *Guide to Ghosts & Haunted Places*, Piatkus LTD, 2001

Underwood P: *Nights in Haunted Houses*, Headline Book Publishing 1994

Underwood P: *The A-Z of British Ghosts*, Chancellor Press, 1992

Underwood P: *This Haunted Isle*, Javelin Books, 1984

Waring E: *Ghosts & Legends of the Dorset Countryside*, Compton Press, 1977

WWW. Paranormaldatabase.com

Index

A

A Farm, North Devon 54

Abbey Church, Bath 17

Abbey Road & Tavy Bridge, Thamesmead Kent 118

Aberdeen 128

Addington, London 118

All Saints Church, Crondall, Berkshire 64

Alma Lane, Crondall, Hampshire 88

Alnwick Castle, Northumbria 82

Alvaston, Derby 71

Ambresbury Hillfort, Essex 18

Ardoch, Perthshire 14

Ardrossan Castle, Ayrshire 33

Arundel, Sussex 71

Attenborough, Nottinghamshire 64

B

B1052, Hadstock, Essex 118

Baconsthorpe Castle, Norfolk 33

Badbury Rings, Dorset 12

Balcombe Railway Tunnel 95

Ballindalloch Castle, Banffshire 92

Balmuto, Fife 92

Bamburgh Castle, Northumbria 34

Battle Abbey, Sussex 34

Bendrose House, Amersham Common, Berkshire 64

Berkley Castle, Gloucestershire 34

Berry Pomeroy Castle, Devon 34

Berwick on Tweed 35

Bestwood Lodge, Nottinghamshire 128

Bethnal Green Tube Station, London 119

Bigg's Cottage, Wash Common 64

Bindon Hill, Dorset 14

Bitterne Manor, Southampton 17

Blackness Castle 36

Blacksmiths Forge Tea Rooms, Pluckley, Kent 54

Blickling Hall 71

Bloodmoor Hill, Suffolk 26

Bodelwyddan Castle, Bodelwyddan 95

Boldre, Hampshire 78

Bolton Priory 36

Bonchester Bridge, Peeblesshire 15

Borley Lodge, Essex 63

Bottlebrush Down, Dorset 12

Bournemouth Town Hall, Dorset 95

Bovington Tank Museum, Dorset 124

Bowerchalke, Wiltshire 15

Bowes, Barnard Castle 18

Bracebridge Hall and Church, Lincolnshire 36

Bradwell on Sea, Essex 18

Bramham Moor, York 36

Brewer Street, London 91

Buckingham Palace, London 101

Buckstones, Yorkshire 54

Burgh Castle, Norfolk 18

Burnham Green, Hertfordshire 26

Burscough Airfield, Lancashire 102

Burton Constable Hall, Hull 15

Burtonwood Old Airfield, Cambridgeshire 103

Burwell Castle, Cambridgeshire 37

Buttsbury, Essex 54

Byward Tower, Tower of London 37

C

Cadover Bridge, Dartmoor 128

Caerleon Campus, Newport 19

Cambridge Airport, Cambridgeshire 103

Cammeringham, Lincolnshire 19

Canvey Island, Essex 30

Carbrook Hall Hotel, Sheffield 65

Carlisle 54

Cassiobury, Hertfordshire 55

Castle Coch, Cardiff 55

Castle Hill, Torrington 71

Castlemilk, Glasgow
Castlemilk, Glasgow 37 98

Chanctonbury Ring, Washington, Sussex 15

Chatwall and Church Stretton, Shropshire 55

Chenies Manor, Buckinghamshire 65

Cheriton, Hampshire 71

Chester 19

Chester Green, Derby 15

Chillingham Castle, Northumbria 37

Chingle Hall, Longridge 19, 38, 56

Christ Church College, Oxford 56

Church Broughton, Derbyshire 119

Church Street, Essex 63

Chysauster, Cornwall 13

Cirencester, Gloucestershire 119

Clacton – on – Sea 120, 128

Cloud's Hill, Bovington, Dorset 96

Coach & Horses Public House, Buckland Brewer, Devon 65

Coal Pit Fields, Bedworth 64

Codnor Castle, Derbyshire 65

College Green, Bristol 128

Colwyn Bay, Wales 119

Conington Railway Junction, Cambridgeshire 125

Coombe Dingle Bridge, Somerset 19

Corbridge, Northumberland 15

Corfe Castle, Dorset 63

Coventry Cathedral, Coventry 119

Croft Castle, Hereford and Worcester 38

Cromarty, Rosshire, Scotland 38

Crossgate, Durham 38

Croydon Aerodrome, London 103

Culloden House 85

D

Dacre Castle, Cumbria 26

Danbury, Essex 17

Dartmoor Prison, Devon 90

Dawlish, Devon 91

Denbigh Moors, Denbigh 19

Dent, Cumbria 30

Dilston, Northumberland 83

Donnington Castle, Berkshire 129

Dover Castle, Kent 20, 56, 88, 125

Dovercourt, Essex 90

Dowsborough, Somerset 30

Duelling Stone at Aylsham 71

Dunnichen, Angus 27

Dunnose Point, The Isle of Wight 92

Dunphail Castle, Nairnshire, Scotland 39

19 Dunraven Street, London 63

Duns Castle, Borders 88

Dunstanburgh Castle, Northumbria 39

Duntrune Castle, Argyll 80

Dunwhich, Suffolk 39

E

East Cowes, Isle of Wight 103

East Stoke, Nottinghamshire 40

East Street, Colchester 63

Edgehill, Vale of the Red Horse, Warwickshire 72

Edwin's Hall, Woodham Ferrers, Essex 56

Eilean Donan Castle 84

F

Faringdon, Berkshire 65

Fauld Crater, Hanbury 125

Feering Church, Essex 93

Fenny Bridges, Devon 40

Flodden Field, Northumbria 40

Ford House, Newton Abbot 79

Fort George, Invernesshire 93

Freezing Hill, Bath 77

Fulwood Barracks, Preston 96

G

Gainsborough Old Hall 30

Garrowby Hill, Stamford Bridge, Yorkshire 120

Gaulden Manor, Somerset 56

George and Dragon Inn, Chester 20

Ghost Hill, Murrow, Cambridgeshire 66

Girton College, Cambridge 20

Gisleham, Suffolk 20

Glen Shiel, Highlands 129

Glencoe, Argyll 80

Glenlivet, Moray 41

Glossop, Derbyshire 16

Golden Hill Fort, Isle of Wight 96

Gop Carn, Trelawnyd 17

Grafton Regis, Northamptonshire 72

Great Pulteney Street, Bath 86

Grenadier Pub, London 88

Gun Hill, Southwold 129

H

Hall Place, Bexley, Kent 41

Hassop, Derbyshire 63

Hayling Avenue, Portsmouth 96

Hedgeley Moor, Northumbria 41

Hendon RAF Museum, London 97

Hengrove Park, Bristol 120

Hermitage Castle, Roxburghshire, Scotland 42

Hermitage Green Lane, Newton le willows, Lancashire 82

Heydon Ditch, Cambridgeshire 27

High Wycombe 66

Hitchin Priory, Hertfordshire 57

Holland House, London 57

Holmsley South Airfield 104

Holy Trinity Church, Goodramgate, York 42

Holy Trinity Churchyard, Wingate, Durham 97

Honeypot Lane, London 16

Hooten Lane, Leigh 129

Hope Valley, Derbyshire 27

Hope, Derbyshire 120

Hopton, Shropshire 72

Horning, Norfolk 27

Hound Tor, Devon 57

Howely Hall, Batley, Yorkshire 66

Huntingdon Castle, Donegal 66

I

IckelsahmVillage Pond, Surrey 97

Imperial War Museum, Duxford, Cambridgeshire 104

Inverary Castle 80

Inverary, Argyll and Bute 129

Inverawe House 87

Iona 30

K

Kidwelly Castle 42

Killiecrankie, Perthshire 81

Kilmington, East Devon 16

Kingley Vale, Sussex 31

Knaresborough, Yorkshire 42

Knighton Gorges, Isle of Wight 43

L

Lake Burwain, Lancashire 66

Lakenheath Airforce Base, Suffolk 104

Lamport, Northamptonshire 120

Landsdown, Somerset 73

Langham Apple Orchard, Norfolk 104

Leap Hill, Northumbria 43

Leicester Guildhall 63

Lewes, Sussex 43

Littlecote Park, Wiltshire 17

Littledean Hall, Forest of Dean 63

Loch Morar near Mallaig 85

Longendale Valley, Derbyshire 121

Lostwithiel, Cornwall 73

Loughton, Essex 67

Lud's Church, Cheshire 43

Ludham Bridge, Norfolk 31

Lustleigh, Devon 44

Lympne Castle, Kent 20

Lyric Bingo Hall 67

M

M11 Southbound, Woodford 121

M6 Toll Road, Lichfield, Staffordshire 21

Maddington Manor, Wiltshire 44

Maghull, Liverpool 73, 85

Malvern Hills, Hereford and Worcester 17

Market Bosworth, Leicestershire 44

Marlpitts Hill, Honiton, Devon 78

Marston Moor, Yorkshire 73

McPhersons Paintworks, Bury 126

Middle Clayden, Buckinghamshire 58

Middleham Castle, Yorkshire 44

Milecastle 42, Hadrian's Wall 21

Mill Hill Barracks, London 129

Mitford Castle, Northumbria 44

Moat Farm, Downham Market, Norfolk 130

Monks Park area, Corsham 21

Montrose Aerodrome, Scotland 105

Moresby Hall, Whitehaven, Cumbria 21, 63, 84

Morwenna Park Estate, Northam 130

N

Neville Castle, Kirkbymoorside 45

Newark Castle 81

Newcastle 45, 58

Newcastle Cathedral 45

Newhouse Inn, Dartmoor 130

North Deans, Lowestoft 126

North Pickenham, Norfolk 105

North Tidworth, Wiltshire 22

North Weald Airbase, Essex 105

O

Old Basing House, Hampshire 74

Old Parsonage, Handforth 85

Oldbury Camp, Wiltshire 17

Otterburn, Northumberland 46

P

Packman Lane, Kiveton Park, Rotherham 16

Paper Hall, Bradford 46

Parham Airfield, Suffolk 106

Pencaet Castle, East Lothian 58

Pengersick Castle, Cornwall 46

Pentland Manor House, London 89

Penwortham Hill, Lancashire 17

Pevensey Castle, Sussex 46

Peveril Castle, Derbyshire 47

Pinocchio's Restaurant, Walton le Dale, Lancashire 67

Pistol Meadow, The Lizard Coastline, Cornwall 47

Pitchford Hall, Somerset 47

Pitreavie Castle 81

Poyntington, Somerset 74

Prestbury, Gloucestershire 59

Prior's Court, Callow End 63

Prudhoe Castle, Northumbria 47

R

RAF Bassingbourne, Cambridgeshire 106

RAF Biggin Hill, Kent 106

RAF Binbrook, Lincolnshire 106

RAF Bircham Newton 107

RAF Bottesford, Leicestershire 107

RAF Bourn, East Anglia 107

RAF Colbey Grange, Lincolnshire 107

RAF Cosford Shropshire 108

RAF Digby, Lincolnshire 108

RAF Driffield, Yorkshire 109

RAF East Kirkby, Lincolnshire 109

RAF Fiskerton, Lincolnshire 109

RAF Grove, Oxfordshire 109

RAF Hawkinge, Kent 110

RAF Hemswell, Lincolnshire 110

RAF Kelstern, Lincolnshire 110

RAF Kimbolton 110

RAF Kirton – in – Linsey, Lincolnshire 111

RAF Leconfield 111

RAF Leeming, Yorkshire 111

RAF Lichfield, Staffordshire 112

RAF Lindholme, Yorkshire 112

RAF Manby, Lincolnshire 113

RAF Mepel, Cambridgeshire 113

RAF Northolt, London 113

RAF Rufforth, Yorkshire 114

RAF Sawbridgeworth 114

RAF Scampton, Lincolnshire 114

RAF Strubby, Lincolnshire 114

RAF Upavon, Wiltshire 97

RAF Valley, Anglesey 17

RAF Waltham, Lincolnshire 114

RAF Welford, Berkshire 115

RAF Wellesbourne Mountford, Warwickshire 115

RAF West Malling, Kent 115

RAF Whitchurch 116

RAF Wickenby, Lincolnshire 116

RAF Wittering, Cambridgeshire 116

Red Lion Square, London 67

Reindeer Inn, Banbury 59

Richborough Castle, Kent 22

Ridgewell Airfield, Essex 117

Ripe Lane, Ripe, Surrey 121

Rock Hall, Northumbria 59

Rolls Royce Factory, Bankfield, Barnoldswick, Lancashire 121

Roman Steps, Llyn Cwm Bychan, Gwynedd 17

Rothiemay Castle 97

Roundway Hill, Wiltshire 75

Rowton, Cheshire 77

Ruthin Castle, Clwyd 48

Ruthven Barracks, Strathspey 48

S

Saddleworth Moor, Rishworth, Lancashire 122

Saint Briavel's Castle, Forest of Dean 48

Salisbury Hall, St Albans 48, 59

Sandbach, Cheshire 75

Scarborough Castle, Yorkshire 48

Senlac Hill, Hastings 49

Shaw Green Lane, Prestbury 49

Slaybrook Corner, Saltwood 22

Somerset House, London 91

South Efford House 130

South Walsham in Norfolk 31

Spanish Head, the Isle of Man 31

St Alban's Church, Fulwood Barracks, Preston 101

St Albans 49

St Andrew's Church, Ashingdon, Essex 28

St Georges Park, York 87

St Lawrence's Church, Alton, Hampshire 75

St Margaret, East Wellow, Hampshire 68

St Mary the Virgin, Kemsing 50

St Mary's Church, Great Baddow, Essex 68

St Nicholas' Cathedral, Newcastle 82

St Nicholas' Church, Brighton 50

St Savour's Church, York 31

Stamford Bridge, Yorkshire 50

Stapleton Woods, Bristol 68

Stone Bridge, Plas Pren 14

Stretton, Cheshire 117

Stubley Old Hall, Derbyshire 87

Sydney Sussex College, Cambridge 68

T

Tangmere Aviation Museum, Surrey 122

Taunton Castle, Somerset 78

Teeside Airport, County Durham 117

The A30 63

The A34 bypass at Newbury 68

The Angel Hotel, Guildford 93

The Battle of Culloden 86

The Battle of Naseby 75

The Binns, West Lothian 60

The Birdcage Inn, Thame 90

The Black Bear Inn, Tewkesbury 50

The Black Swan Public House, Bow Road, London 98

The Capricorn Club, Brightstone, Isle of Wight 122

The Castle of Mey, Caithness, Scotland 126

The Castle Public House 22

The Channel Islands 136

The Chequers, Smarden 90

The Chough Hotel, Chard 50

The Coliseum, St Martin's Lane, London 98

The County Assembly Rooms, Lincoln 64

The County Hotel, Dumfries 86

The Crab and Lobster, Sidlesham 60

The Cross Keys, Saffron Walden, Essex 69

The Crown and Raven Hotel, Somerset 61

The Dales, Ipswich 22

The Dun Cow, Shrewsbury 61

The Eagle Hotel, King's Lynn, Norfolk 122

The Falstaff Public House 130

The Fire brigade Headquarters, Bristol 51

The Fisheries Inn, London 63

The George Tavern, Strand 63

The Globe, Ludlow 51

The Goat Inn, Strumpshaw, Norfolk 127

The Golden Fleece Public House, York 122

The Golden Lion, St Ives 69

The Governor's House, Bridgnorth 76

The Green Dragon Alehouse, Waltham Abbey 63

The Gun Tavern, London 92

The Heddon Oak, Somerset 78

The High Street, Holme Hale, Norfolk 131

The Hippo Club 64

The Imphal Barracks, Fulford 93

144

The King Charles Parlour Public House, Wells 64

The King's Arms, Peckham Rye, London 123

The King's Head Hotel, Cirencester 63

The King's Head Public House, Cullompton, Devon 123

The Kings Manor, York 76

The Langham Hotel, London 98

The Leather Exchange Public House, Leathermarket Street, London 123

The Lyric Theatre, Shaftesbury Avenue, London 98

The Mermaid Public House, Colchester 63

The Naval and Military Club, Picadilly, London 123

The Naval Dockyard, Plymouth 131

The New Forest 51

The Old Court House, Newent 63

The Old Mitre Inn, Farnham 131

The Old School Cottages, Bromley Cross 61

The Old Sun Inn, Saffron Walden, Essex 69

The Old Vicarage, Grantchester 99

The Olde Rock House, Barton on Irewell 61

The Olde Starr Inn, York 76

The Petwood Hotel, Woodhal Spa, Lincolnshire 124

The Queen Anne Block, Royal Naval College 87

The Rake Inn, Rochdale 69

The Ridgeway 17

The Ring O' Bells, Middleton 62

The River View Park Estate, Gravesend, Kent 124

The Roman Walls, Chester 63

The Rovers Return Trinket Shop, Shudehill, Manchester 86

The Royal British Legion, Brixham 91

The Salmon Inn, Northumbria 62

The Salutation Inn, Nottingham 69

The Schooner Hotel, Alnmouth 131

The Skirrid Mountain Inn, Abergaveny 70

The Stork Hotel, Billinge 62

The Strood, Mersea Island, Essex 23

The Swan Inn, Romsey, Hampshire 70

The Theatre Royal, Winchester, Hampshire 99

The Tomb of the Unknown Soldier, Westminster Abbey 99

The Towy Valley, Dyfed, Wales 124

The TSW Studio's, Plymouth 89

The White Swan Pub, Newbury 99

Theydon Bois Hillfort, Epping Forest 23

Thor's Cave, Derbyshire 23

Three Crowns Hotel, Chagford 63

Tower Field, Flamborough Castle 51

Treasue Holt, Essex 63

Treasurer's House, York 23

Turweston Airfield, Northamptonshire 117

Tutt Hill, Suffolk 32

W

Waltham Abbey 63

Wardour Castle, Wiltshire 76

Washington Airport, Sunderland 118

Wath Wood Hospital, Wath upon Dearne, Yorkshire 24

Weare Gifford Hall, Devon 52

Wecock Farm, Hampshire 17

West Tump Barrow 13

Westonzoyland, Somerset 79

Wheel Cottage, Thundersley 94

Wheston Hall, Derbyshire 70

Who'd Have Thought It, Milton Coombe 63

Wig and Pen Club, the Strand, London 70

Windmill House 131

Windsor Castle, London 101

Winnington Bridge, Northwhich, Cheshire 76

Winter's Armoury, Essex 63

Woodbridge Bar, Woodbridge, Suffolk 124

Woodchester Mansion, Stroud 24

Woodcroft Manor, Peterborough 77

Wroxham, Norfolk 24

Y

Ye Olde Trip to Jerusalem, Nottingham 52

York between Church Street and Davygate 25

Lightning Source UK Ltd.
Milton Keynes UK
UKHW01f1815020918
328218UK00001B/215/P